D0214314

TALKING ABOUT LITERACY

Principles and Practice of Adult Literacy Education

Jane Mace

London and New York

First published in 1992
by Routledge
11 New Fetter Lane, London EC4P 4EE

Simultaneously published in the USA and Canada
by Routledge
a division of Routledge, Chapman and Hall Inc.
29 West 35th Street, New York, NY 10001

© 1992 Jane Mace

Typeset in Garamond by Laserscript Limited, Mitcham, Surrey
Printed and bound in Great Britain by
Mackays of Chatham PLC, Chatham, Kent

British Library Cataloguing in Publication Data
A catalogue record for this book is available from the British Library.

Library of Congress Cataloging in Publication Data
Mace, Jane.
  Talking about literacy: principles and practice of adult literacy
  education/Jane Mace.
  p. cm.
  Includes bibliographical references and index.
  ISBN 0–415–08044–4. – ISBN 0–415–06655–7 (pbk.)
  1. Functional literacy – Great Britain. 2. Reading (Adult Education)
  – Great Britain. I. Title.
LC156.G7M28 1992
374′.012 – dc20   91-41608
                                                                     CIP

ISBN 0–415–08044–4
0–415–06655–7 (pbk)

to Jessica and Joe

CONTENTS

ACKNOWLEDGEMENTS

Towards the end of working on this book I went, partly out of writer's procrastination, to an event on a Friday evening. As it turned out, that event gave me more new energy than any amount of poring over drafts. It was an evening to celebrate International Literacy Day (8 September). A group of twelve people (students and two tutors) sat round in a room in South-east London and listened as three of them read and spoke about their writing. To those three, and the determination and eloquence of the whole group, I owe the inspiration to finish what I began. Beyond them are the many adult students who have participated in literacy education with me, without whom I would have had nothing to say in the first place, and just a few of whom are featured in the book.*

The best advice I found from another writer was Dorothea Brande's stricture to the writer to treat her writing desk as a workbench. (If you start daydreaming or fretting, get up and go somewhere else. The place where you have your writing equipment is the place where you write.) Other advisers to whom I turned in difficult moments included Frank Smith, Sue Roe and Natalie Rothenberg. I have never met any of them. Three friends, however, gave me help of other kinds, and I would like to thank them here. First, Ruth Lesirge, with whom I have shared travel, laughter and some hard times, and who combined direct questions with affirmative warmth in her comments on drafts. Second, Wendy Moss who taught me again how to keep a sense of humour about serious matters and restated some of my muddled thought in intelligible language. And third, Rodney Mace, with whom I have lived for nearly twenty-five years, and who gave me the same encouragement and faith that he has always given me when I have had difficult things to face.

Discussions with the group of colleagues in the Diploma in Literacy and Adult Learning, and at numerous conferences over the years, have certainly influenced and inspired some of the thinking in the book. I also recall with appreciation the forty or more staff and tutors with whom, over eleven years, I have worked at the Lee Community Education Centre. (The day after we finally closed the building in July 1991 was the day I sat down to write this.)†

Thanks, finally, to two other people: to Jay Edwards, weaver, who taught me the basics of weaving and helped me to prepare the warp for a rug at the beginning of the book, so that I could turn, when the writing got stuck, to the texture and colour of yarn on the loom; and to Helen Fairlie, my editor, who kept her nerve and her confidence in the project when I changed the book proposal from a 'practical' one to a more theoretical one.

Jane Mace
October 1991

* I have only used the full names of students in the book when they have fully given their permission for me to do so; which means, when their writing appears in a publication intended for a readership beyond the group they belong to. I have not, therefore, given the full names of those writers in courses I have taught with a publication of thirty copies or less or those people with whom I have not been able to re-check my use of an interview transcript with them.

† The Lee Community Education Centre opened in 1973 as an outpost of the adult studies programme of Goldsmiths' College, London. In 1989 the College authorities made the decision that it had to close, on the grounds that the work of community education and literacy was no longer justifiable in its new funding arrangements as a university institution. Closure was delayed by a year as a result of considerable protest. July 1991 saw its end as a centre of this kind; the building was put on the open market, but at the time of writing is still empty and unsold. For convenience, I refer to it in this book by its short title, by which it remains best known: the Lee Centre.

INTRODUCTION

TO THE READER

There are three things I want to say to you about this book.

1 The reader: how I see you.

First, the subject of this book I hope is interesting to anyone, not only those who teach adults. It is (at least it is intended to be) a book for those people, certainly; but it is also for anyone interested in thinking about their own, as well as in promoting other people's, *critical and confident reading and writing.*

The term 'adult literacy education' means the education of people who have an interest in wanting to be able to read and write better. That is a different, and larger, constituency than was conceived of in the 'adult literacy campaign' of the early 1970s in the UK. The people on whose behalf that was launched were those who could barely read and write at all and who were seen as having a 'need' to read and write for everyday life. In this book, I am discussing the principles at work in the education of those who often can read, but wish they could read better; who, technically, can put writing on paper, but have a desire to do so with more expression and coherence. The people I am thinking about, therefore, are people who have made a decision that they have a sufficient interest in their own literacy to choose to engage with others in an education designed to develop it.

The difference between the two ideas lies in two respects: first, I am discussing people with a declared interest rather than an ascribed need; and second, I am extending the notion of literacy as 'basic' education to one which includes a repertoire of purposes and contexts for reading and writing.

xi

This understanding of 'adult literacy education' means that I have written this book with an idea of you, the readers, as people who may be working in any one of the following areas:

Community education.
Employment training, and work with unemployed people.
Women's education.
Access to higher education.
Language and literacy policy development.
Writing development generally.
Literacy research.

All these are concerned with the education of people with an interest in their own literacy development.

At the same time, you may be someone interested simply in seeing how the processes of your own literacy education might relate to policies and thinking about the phenomenon of 'illiteracy' in a society which sees itself as 'literate'.

2 Literacy: why bother about it?

The second thing is this: I have come to think that we who organise programmes of literacy education for adults (in the broad sense I have indicated above) have to be more convincing about its advantages, and less pushed into promoting it only as a job ticket. What are its pleasures? Why do we think that it is an activity worth anyone's time? Have we not all taken it too much for granted, that literacy is a desirable thing to work for? All the publicity efforts of the 1970s to persuade the 'adult illiterate' that she or he could shed a burden of hidden shame and discover new confidence in literacy was built on the assumption that everyone must want literacy and felt bad if they didn't have it. The very word 'campaign' assumed it. I was among those who thought it was obvious.

A few years ago I started to question this assumption. In 1983 and 1986 (and later, in 1990/91), I was commissioned to promote and publicise courses designed to provide a literacy opportunity which would entail no extra cost to the prospective student of their time and money. The courses would be free, in time during which they would already be at work; they would be paid to attend. In both cases, a good number of people made the decision to join these courses. However, despite the apparent attractions of the course arrangement, I also met with some people who agreed they couldn't spell, didn't feel up to reading all they might want to, but didn't want the course anyway.[1]

Admittedly, these were a very small minority of those I spoke to; and some didn't let me know either way, using comments like, 'Let the younger ones go, dear; I'm too old for that sort of thing'. But it was enough for me to review my own assumptions and start a process of questioning the principles by which I and others set about promoting and teaching literacy to adults.

Nearly two decades on from the 'adult literacy campaign', the question 'why literacy?' now seems in urgent need of new discussion. A vast literature exists on the ways and means of ensuring that children leave school in possession of an ability to read and write; yet adult and community education programmes across the country testify that a large (and changing) adult population continues to be without the literacy education it wants and needs. The chorus of claims of a decline in literacy standards in this country reached a new crescendo in 1990 with the 'real books' debate;[2] in the same year, the UN's work to promote International Literacy Year called for renewed action across the world (including in so-called 'developed' countries) to establish adequate literacy education opportunities.[3]

If such programmes are to succeed, however, they have to be persuasive as to the positive benefits of literacy; for, although many people may not have the ability to read and write confidently, it appears that not all of those people find these programmes attractive. The most recent national study of literacy in this country, in 1987[4] reported two key revelations: one, that there were more people (13 per cent) who found literacy hard than the earlier campaign figure (of 6 per cent) had suggested; and two, that an extremely small number of these people (only 1 in 10) were actually taking part in any education to make literacy easier for themselves. The interviews on which this study was based had been carried out, not in 1961, before any major national effort to promote adult literacy had got off the ground, but in 1981, nearly ten years after the first publicity about adult literacy in this country. The question then arises: could it be that some of those not coming to classes knew about those classes, could afford the time and money to attend them, but did not want to join them?

A year after the publication of the 1987 study, I was involved in a smaller one, carried out by a group of literacy students themselves, which revealed something else: most of their peers with whom they discussed their research question, 'How do people decide to come to a literacy class?' had thought about coming for many years before actually joining a class.[5] This finding suggests at least one other question: what made them decide against joining a class for all that time? It's possible that the answer could be: they had thought about coming to such a class, but had never before had any information about such a class actually existing in a place or at a time that would have been practical for them. It's also possible that they had thought about joining a class for many years, but had not joined one, even though there had been a well-publicised centre in their locality, because they did not want to.

A study of sixty-eight adult literacy students carried out in 1976/77 had already contained some indications of these possibilities; but it wasn't until I reread it more recently that I focused clearly on the section on 'drop outs' (people who came along to literacy schemes, but did not return after a first interview or meeting with their tutor) and noticed the authors' suggestion that 'dropping out' of literacy education could be attributed to a positive interest in other things than literacy. (It reminded me, too, of an abbreviation we used in the record-keeping of the literacy scheme where I worked at the time: DTU – didn't turn up – and I discuss this further in Part I, chapter 1.)[6]

Why, after all, should it be so attractive for an adult with a lot of other things to do on their Thursday evenings, or Monday mornings, or whenever it is, to spend time learning to read and write better? 'Functional literacy' programmes have long been promoted in this and other countries as a means to employment. Yet plenty of people who can read and write do not have jobs and have no immediate prospect of getting one. (In addition, research in this country[7] has indicated that the need to be able to read and write for many jobs may not in any case be as great as the employer's job selection procedures indicate.) Literacy for employment, in reality, comprises many kinds of literacy, depending on the job, the organisation and the economic context of the work; and what an employer thinks they may need their employees to be able to read and write at work may not be what those people think they want to be able to do. The full range of literacy purposes and possibilities available to any of us has barely been described, let alone promoted. And while the benefits of literacy remain vague, the disadvantages and difficulty of investing time in acquiring it are sometimes overpowering.

Just as it is not obvious how it benefits an individual, it is not always obvious that literacy, in itself, benefits the society as a whole. Michael Clanchy argued in 1979:

> Anthropological studies of non-literate societies in the third world and sociological studies of deprived urban proletariats in the west both suggest that *literacy in itself is primarily a technology. It has different effects according to circumstances and is not a civilizing force in itself*[my italics].[8]

In all that I have said so far, I do not for a moment want to give the impression that I am dismissing the undoubted pain and frustration of many individuals and groups who cannot read and write in the dominant language of a society regarding itself as literate. My interest is in trying to find something other than a problem-solution reflex to the issue (the problem is illiteracy: the solution is more literacy). The question I set out to discuss in this book is: what other ways are open to us of talking about literacy than as a solution to 'the problem of illiteracy'?

3 Reading, writing and principles.

The third point concerns the subtitle of the book. It's a book about practice (that is, teaching practice), but it aims to be more than a book about 'methods'. The intention has been to identify, from practice, some *principles* by which a certain kind of literacy teaching practice is guided.

By no means all literacy teaching practice falls within this framework; and I have no wish to suggest that the five principles I have identified are absolute and universal ones. Rather, by rereading my own and other people's accounts of teaching practice, I have picked out what seem to me to be the five most persistent themes and intentions within the ideas being suggested in these accounts.

All writing is a journey. Since I wrote my first book on literacy[9] I have published articles and reports, a book offering 'discussion and materials' for teaching,[10] and two other jointly edited books.[11] I have also gained more experience of attempting to persuade people into courses which are designed to encourage them to write: attempts which also required all sorts of writing from me – letters, leaflets, worksheets, and evaluation reports of these courses. Both the published writing and the publicity work I have found to be concerned with principles of *context, equality, authorship* and *community.*

It was in the more recent experience of designing and teaching, with a colleague, an academic course for literacy educators that I had the opportunity to focus on and reaffirm, in addition, the principle of *inquiry*. The movement since 1984 in this country towards a closer relationship between research and practice in adult literacy work undoubtedly gave me confidence in a sense of there being a large number of colleagues also concerned with this.[12]

Until undertaking the particular journey of writing this book, however, I had not described any of this in terms of principles. Yet, insistently, in all this writing, reading and discussion with colleagues and students, the same question kept recurring for me: how do we explain to our students (or those people we wish to persuade to become students) what our own thinking is behind the literacy work we propose that they should do? The five principles proposed are my own attempt at one such explanation.

Uses of literacy are enormously varied and often deeply contradictory. This is why, I repeat, these five principles should not be read as having a universal intention. There is, however, one thread which links them all: namely, the effort to re-establish writing as central to literacy education. Other writers have pointed out the social forces against this effort. It has been pointed out, for example, that reading is in asymmetrical relationship to writing; that we read more than we write; and that 'reading can do without writing, but writing cannot do without reading'.[13] It has also been suggested that few people write habitually and for pleasure.[14] The 'imposed' literacy of our education and cultural experience after primary school largely concerns the reading of other people's writing.[15] Anything which concerns writing for imaginative or reflective purposes belongs to an area of adult life called 'leisure' (which, in terms of funding, belongs on the very edges of serious education for adults).[16] The original literacy campaign itself was launched under the demand for a 'right to read'.

All this suggests a popular and institutional view of literacy as having, most of all, to do with reading. There remains a paradox. While society expects all of us to read, and prefers most of us to keep writing to a minimum, the ability to compose thought on paper is more than ever central to the mechanisms of awarding qualifications at the end of a course of study or training. We are a society which, above all else, requires written evidence of learning and skills. Literacy education with adults who do not have such qualifications cannot avoid, then, teaching something about writing. This teaching can stop short at the point of teaching techniques for 'correct' writing. The principles of context, inquiry, authorship, equality and community aspire to take the task of writing beyond these limits; for they are grounded in a view that literacy education means persuading adult students that they are writers as well as readers, that they have an entitlement to be read, as well as to read others. Literacy education, on this basis, means a journey towards confident, critical and active authorship; for authorship embraces both reading and writing.

principles & purpose

ON WRITING BOOKS

Writing from the inside out

In order to discuss this idea in this book, and the principles with which it is interwoven, I found I first had to deal with my own struggle as a writer in writing it. At the heart of this struggle is the old writer's enemy, the voice in my head which, at regular intervals, interrupted the writing with the terrible question: what makes you think you have anything to say? (Others have already said it; they have said it so much better; why should anyone be interested in what you have to add?) Sometimes there is no answer, and the best thing to do is to go for a walk or clean the windows. At other times, the only answer appears to be to give up the effort altogether. At these moments, I have found comfort and encouragement in Andrea Loewenstein's words about her view of the writing teacher. On her approach to teaching women in prison, she said:

> For me, becoming a writer meant beginning to write from the center of myself. Many writing teachers tend to teach from the outside in instead of from the inside out. 'Writing well,' we are told again and again, 'is not magic. It has nothing to do with inspiration. It is a skill which can and must be learned.' While there is a certain truth to this (especially after the initial stage), to deny the magic, the inspiration part of our process, is to force it into a sterile mold . . .
>
> Writing, when taught from the inside out, is a process by which a woman's magical, creative ability is tapped. My job is not to 'teach her to write'. Instead, our job together is to allow her to find what it is she needs to say and how to say it.[17]

To teach others this 'writing from the inside out', it is our job to do so ourselves. There are many distractions from the effort to find and to keep a centre to write from: but benefits to the writer there certainly are. Seeing our writing is also to see our thinking; reading it suggests new writing and other thinking pathways. Much of this thought is otherwise compressed inside the head, 'unthought-out'. Andrea Loewenstein argues that 'learning to write is part of the more important process of learning that one is not invisible'. Of all the possible benefits of literacy education, this seems to me one of the most attractive. This is not the book I thought it would be when I first proposed it, or later began to write it; I have gained inspiration from others and, occasionally, had moments of magic in the process of that kind of writing which entails stitching together arguments I had not previously seen as connected.

Writing, shop pies and tinned food

It was in a collection of stories written about boys and (so the publishers said, at any rate) for boys, that I found the story of a woman who found what she wanted to say;[18] not, as in Andrea Lowenstein's account, in the context of a group with a sympathetic teacher, but alone. Her journey to become a writer begins with a resistance to literacy. Introduced as 'the best housewife in Clegg Row', Maggie Gregory is described as a proud wife and mother, who had her doorstep scrubbed first thing in the morning, washing on the line before the children went off to school, and 'the best-stocked kitchen in the neighbourhood'. Maggie, however, shocks the the new rector by revealing that she never learned to read. '"A fine respectable wife and mother like yourself, ma'am" he said, "that can't understand the written word no more than some misfortunate heathen!"' She explains that, as the only girl, she had got 'stuck with the housework' after her mother died, and adds that she has no regrets 'when I see some of them as have been educated'. The priest insists that she 'must' learn to read. Reluctantly, she agrees to the rector giving her twelve-year-old son the job of teaching her. In a fortnight, after his coaxing, bullying and cajoling, she learns to read the sentence 'Tom filled his can at the well'.

That, as far as the priest was concerned, had achieved all the literacy Maggie as a 'respectable woman' needed. Things do not quite go according to plan, however. For once she has overcome her initial resistance to literacy, there's no stopping Maggie. The boy, Timothy, calls his father in alarm, crying that she is 'reading away like mad an' won't stop'. Harry, his father, recognises a revolution when he sees one: 'Her were the best wife in the row, but God only knows where this'll end.' The housework gets neglected. Maggie is constantly reading; she is found 'sneaking off to the public library every morning with a book hidden away in her shopping-basket'. The doorstep does not get cleaned till Saturday afternoon. Meals are burnt, or consist of shop pies and tinned food. Maggie has even 'stooped as low as buying ready-peeled potatoes'.

The priest, accosted by a now desperate Harry, says it is 'too late to unteach her, but no home could go on like this'; and hits upon the idea of a 'reading day'. Maggie is to be rationed to reading only one day a week. Every Thursday, Harry makes her breakfast in bed and she goes on reading till noon. In the afternoon, she sits on the bench in the churchyard, reading. The family, quiet in the evening while she reads on, 'certainly knew her worth now; at one time they had taken everything she did for them for granted'.

The climax of this short tale is Maggie's announcement one evening that she has had enough of books, as she 'could write better herself'. Harry and Timothy return from another visit to the priest who this time has no suggestions, saying only: 'We must accept the fact that your wife is a very remarkable woman.' The ending is a gentle celebration of their acceptance:

> Father and son walked home in silence. As they walked into Clegg Row, Harry looked at Timothy and thought he detected a glint of pride in the boy's eye.
> 'Huh' was all he said.
> 'Washing-up's waiting, Dad', said Timothy. 'Shall we get down to it?'
> 'This book'll take her years', said his father with a sigh.
> 'If it's like her cooking and her baking, Dad, it will be well worth waiting for.'[19]

Fiction has a way of expressing the drama of education in a way that textbooks like this one cannot. This story, first published in 1961, is a delightful parable of literacy and liberation. (I have never cleaned my front steps and my household is used to my erratic contributions to cooking; nevertheless, the activity of writing a book certainly made me a more antisocial person to live with than usual. For anyone curious to compare their experiences of writing with mine, I have described, in the Afterword, something of what the writing of this one taught me.)

THE SHAPE OF THIS BOOK

This is a book about teaching, but I have preferred the term 'literacy worker' or 'literacy educator' to that of 'teacher', precisely because this work entails more than classroom teaching. There are enormous emotional and political associations with literacy, as there are not always with other subjects. The job of the literacy educator, like it or not, has to do with attitudes. Her work is about changing attitudes and challenging prejudices – whether in the form of publicity strategies or seminars for community workers, in counselling new students or in broadcast interviews on local education opportunities. In short, adult literacy education means not only teaching courses like 'fresh start', 'basic skills', 'study skills' 'communication skills' 'language support' and 'return to study', but also designing strategies to encourage people to see that these courses may meet their own interests – and educating them and others to rethink their own attitudes to 'illiteracy'.

Part I of the book, then, addresses two issues that concern me in this last area of work: the issues of representation and truth in my own and other people's talk and writing about literacy. The first chapter, 'Problems of representation', discusses some of the problems in attempting to describe and report on other people's literacy experience – whether in the social category of 'illiterate' or the educational one of 'students'; and distinguishes between the individual portrait and that of a group. The second, 'The truth for now', links the issue of representation in writing to the anxiety for 'truth' in writing about our own experience and history, and suggests that an acceptance of partial truths is essential for any writer.

Part II discusses the five principles that I have picked out from practice in literacy work: principles of *context, inquiry, authorship, equality* and *community.* The sequence follows, to an extent, the chronology of thinking in developing programmes of education, and could be read as such, namely:

Context: the internal, local, and social/political context of the course being promoted and negotiated.

Inquiry: the process of continuing dialogue within the first stage of a course, in which students contribute to the ideas for practical work to develop the first stages of their writing.

Authorship: early draft composition, situations for private and informal writing practice.

Equality: the writing develops; students reveal their work to each other and acquire a sense of themselves as readers and editors of their own and each others' writing.

Community: some links between the classroom work and the relationships beyond it – in workplaces and elsewhere; and the creative tensions between personal and collective learning.

The third chapter, 'Listening to the questions', discusses the principle of *context* in the promotion of literacy courses and opportunities; the context of the literate in promoting literacy; and the distinction between a search for 'needs' and one for 'interests' in literacy, illustrated with examples of outreach and promotion work.

In the fourth, 'The teacher-researcher', I try to relate the researching stance of the outreach worker with a principle of *inquiry* adopted by a researching rather than instructing teacher. As teacher-researchers, I suggest, we learn to give some meaning to the much-used concept of 'student-centred learning', and enable the students to be participants in a research project of their own making; using and extending their own experience and developing the range of vocabulary with which they want to express it.

The fifth chapter, 'Authors and identity', discusses the use of autobiographical writing in literacy teaching, and the ways in which both the rights and responsibilities of *authorship* can be shared. There are, I suggest, ways in which students' belief in themselves as authors may be affirmed by small-scale publishing of their writing.

'Readers equal writers' picks out the fourth principle of *equality*, and discusses strategies by which inexperienced readers may reverse the prevailing sense of inequality between themselves and the published writers they read, and learn strength in themselves as their own readers and editors. This chapter assumes that some draft writing has already begun, and suggests how, by ensuring that there is an explicit commitment to equality, student writers can recognise their own powers as critical readers of these drafts, and in so doing, take a constructively critical view of other writers.

Finally, in 'Vocations and vocationalism' I examine the principle of *community*, and ways in which methods and styles of insignificant communications can have significance for a sense of common purpose. I contrast a concept of 'the workplace community' with an individualised model of literacy as a means to an employment career-path in a competitive world, and discuss alternative understandings of vocational purposes for literacy learning.

Part I

ISSUES

1

PROBLEMS OF REPRESENTATION

The question of how to define and describe literacy can be fascinating or interminable, depending on the mood you happen to be in. A library of literature exists on the subject. Its opposite, illiteracy, has been the subject of national campaigns, dedicated to its 'eradication'. No one has yet proposed a universal formula to achieve this: but for some time the 'literacy' which would replace it was assumed to be capable of single definition. Fortunately, there is an increasing agreement in studies of literacy that such a definition is not possible. Not only, these studies suggest, do societies vary, but also there is in any society a plurality of literacies at work.

The issue of how we define and describe *illiteracy* is, in my view, also problematic – particularly in an industrialised country like Britain, where we pride ourselves on a universal system of primary and secondary education. It is problematic because the idea of illiteracy, in our culture, is one associated with strong emotions. Illiteracy, depending on who is thinking about it, raises feelings of shock, contempt, disbelief, anger, shame and pity. Representations of the illiterate by the literate are therefore likely to be highly charged with one or more of these emotions.

The campaign for literacy was carried out by the literate, on behalf of people defined as 'adult illiterate'. In this chapter I discuss the problem this raises of representation[1] for campaigners, or advocates for literacy, speaking and writing about what it is like not to be able to read and write, and arguing the rights of the illiterate – on their behalf – to adequate education. The early arguments for national attention to adult illiteracy in this country were infused with an aid mentality: the illiterate in Britain were a third world in our midst, a blot on the national conscience, who deserved and should be given help. More recently, this mentality has been overtaken by

3

the rhetoric of a market economy: the illiterate hold back our economic stability, and must be trained in enough literacy to ensure that they meet the demands of an economy seen to be in a state of unprecedented change.

For literacy educators, it has taken effort to assert an alternative agenda to those of aid and economics: namely, the agenda of inequality and class. Our jobs and our programmes depend on using the language of the dominant ideology. To reaffirm the political realities of illiteracy, we depend on the collective energies of our students: rarely indeed do such energies gain space in public media to represent their experience for themselves.

In this chapter I first describe one example of this public, first-hand representation, 'Liberating literacy'. Next, I contrast this with the language used by me and others from a position of seeing 'the illiterate as someone else'. The use of oral interview transcripts is then compared to that of written 'evidence' by published literacy students, 'authors and interviewees', which, I suggest, offers a more complex account than a simple story of the illiterate achieving their life's ambition to become literate and live happily ever after. 'Describe or quantify?' raises the problem of how to reconcile the need to argue for scarce resources in cost-benefit terms with this more complex understanding of literacy's benefits. Finally, I compare alternative representations of an interest in literacy education, 'authentic voices'.

LIBERATING LITERACY

This was the name of a film made as a contribution to International Literacy Year, and first screened by Channel 4 in December 1990.[2] There are seven main participants: Paulo Freire, the Brazilian educator and author of a number of books on literacy and liberation, and six people who, at some stage in their lives, had been literacy students; Corinne Shires, Peter Goode, Edie Woolie, John Glynn, Virginia McLean and John Paul. The programme showed us nine scenes in which people (in one scene, children; in the rest, adults) were engaged in literacy education as learners: a primary school, a work-based course, a job club, a prison, a student-run basic education college, a women's centre, an open-learning centre, a history class, and a community publishing group's class and then publication party.

There were several unusual features of the programme, among others:

(a) it told us about, not a single version of literacy, or a single context for adult literacy work, but eight different contexts and interpretations of adult literacy work in England and Scotland; and

(b) the six people (other than Paulo Freire) were presented, not in studio interview as examples of individual martyrs to illiteracy, nor as heroic achievers against the odds, but as reporters, with (as the narrator put it) 'a specific insight into literacy'. The producer, Colin Thomas, filmed the six in Britain and then took the film to São Paolo in Brazil for Paulo Freire to add his contribution. At intervals throughout the programme, we saw Paulo Freire in a studio control room and heard his comment on the section that we, as viewers, had just watched with him. At the end of the programme we saw the group of six watching him on screen making his commentary; and heard their comments about his.

It would be wrong to suggest that this was a film made either by illiterates or by students of literacy; and naïve to imagine that editorial power resided with them. However, precisely because so much of the public image of the illiterate has been stereotyped, the programme was impressive for the role it gave to the six reporters. One by one, they talked to an interviewer about their experience of attitudes to illiteracy. Then, one by one, they reported on their own or other people's literacy education. Edie Woolie, for example, visited an open-learning centre and a women's centre. Virginia McLean took us into a GCSE English class and the Black Makers of History group she belonged to. Peter Goode visited a class in a prison and then read the poetry he had written and published with Pecket Well Basic Education College, of which he is a member.

Colleagues who have viewed the film have commented that several of the eight scenes of literacy education it depicted actually perpetuate an image of the passive literacy learner being controlled by very limited methods of teaching literacy. The commentary given to these scenes by the reporters was restrained; but their critical reading of what they saw was unquestionably there. John Glynn visited a literacy job club. With him, we watched a man in a class attempting to match a word on a slip of paper in his hand with one of the list of words on a flipchart in front of him. We listened to the instructor urging him on. John's comment afterwards was simply: 'As important in learning to read is building confidence; and that, to me, does the opposite.'

Edie Woolie's reaction to the room of computers at the open learning centre was this:

> You'd have never got me in here five years ago. If you're going to educate people for work you're going to educate them for a false idea because there's no such thing as work these days. So you're educating them just to keep them quiet.

Peter Goode, speaking of his visit to the prison education class said:

> To go into somewhere that, to me, is enforced security and be insecure, and to go in a place where everything is run by an authority and be disarmed, and to actually believe that people can find education in this environment was exciting, yet very very threatening. It was horrible. And yet I was speaking and talking to people who were actually gaining strength through that.

The programme began with a clip from each of the six participants in interview, each speaking about the experience of illiteracy at school. (John Glynn: 'What I remember was just horrific. I felt I just got a little bit behind and that just seemed to snowball'; Corinne Shires: 'One situation was when I had a hat on, a cone hat, and it had a big D on; and I had to stand in a corner with it on me head.') Literacy parables on the media have often begun with such accounts of individual misery; often, too, they have gone on to tell how the individuals then achieved new-found confidence – as individuals.

This programme showed something different. In one scene, we watched Corinne Shires stitch an embroidered poem she had written into a huge patchwork, on which other people were working at the same time. It was the collective creation of Pecket Well College, of which she, like Peter Goode, is a member. Towards the end, we caught two other glimpses of this sense of group membership. John Paul, of the Edinburgh history group in which we saw him participating earlier in the programme, said: 'It's made me feel I belonged to Scotland, and I've got to help other people to believe their identity.' Virginia McLean, who we earlier saw in a wonderfully joyful scene of celebration at the publishing party for the Black Makers of History book to which she contributed, said this, of its attempts to fund-raise for the project's future: 'We are determined that it must go forwards.'

To sum up so far: this film, in my view, is a rare example of a representation by people 'with a special insight into literacy' of their own and other people's experiences, not only of gaining a confidence in their own literacy, but of changing their sense of identity from one of individual failure to that of a collective strength. In the next three sections, I discuss the problems raised by representations of illiterates and their literacy achievements made (to reverse Andrea Loewenstein's position on writing) 'from the outside in'.

THE ILLITERATE AS SOMEONE ELSE

Literacy teachers, answering the anxious questions; Who *are* these people? how do they cope? have to remember our own discoveries of 'illiteracy'. Many of us also once thought that 'people-who-can't-read-and-write' were other, alien people. The education of the literate requires us to apply the same patience with others as we have learned to use with our own past selves.

The answers we can give call on two things: our own memory, and our listener's imagination. We appeal to remembered knowledge of the people who have become our students; and to the listener's imagination – of how they would themselves manage, without literacy, the reading and writing desires and demands of daily life. Indeed, much of the content of tutor training courses in this country has used these two strategies: to quote from the testimony of those who have become literacy students, and to role-play the feelings they report about the experience of illiteracy.

There is, however, a third strategy: namely, to invite the literate participants to articulate the limits of their own literacy – and in so doing, to recognise the continuum of illiteracy–literacy we all inhabit. The fact that this invitation was increasingly to be found in tutor and staff training in the 1980s, I think, had to do with several changes in the experience of teachers and trainers; among others:

1 The pattern of adult literacy work had moved from the model of one-to-one (student:volunteer tutor), which was dominant at the start of this work in the early 1970s, to that of the group, with a paid teacher. (By 1987 the Adult Literacy and Basic Skills Unit (ALBSU) reported that 83 per cent of the 110,000 students in basic education were learning in groups; but was careful to point out that 'what is deemed to constitute a group differs from authority to authority. In some cases groups consist of a number of students taught individually by a volunteer tutor under the supervision of a paid tutor.'[3]

7

2 The movement in women's education and women's liberation had inspired a number of women teachers and educators, with experience of literacy work, to develop 'fresh start' courses for women, coinciding with a 'return to study' move for mature students generally with the aim of providing access opportunities to higher education.[4] The constituency for these courses was described, not in terms of literacy deficit, but in the language of positive discrimination. Women applying to these courses, certainly, commonly described themselves as 'no good at' spelling; but the courses explicitly set out to encourage them to believe, not only that they would get positive help with their reading and writing, but also that this sense of personal deficiency could be seen as a product of systematic discrimination against women's power and knowledge. The gains reported by women attending these courses referred to the mutual support of a group. As regards the illiteracy/literacy opposition, the distinction between someone declaring themselves unable to read and write at all, and someone else saying they were no good at these things made a cut-and-dried distinction between illiteracy and literacy even more inappropriate.

These moves were in contrast to much of the adult literacy publicity in the 1970s, which used the term 'adult illiterate', illustrated the 'progress' made in terms of measurable reading ages (together with some stories of increased personal confidence), described the causes in terms of individual histories of interrupted or unequal opportunities, and gave examples which were, in the majority, male. In such writing, I include my own.[5] More sensational versions of this set of images were to be found, of course, in the local and national press. The casual readers of newspapers were invited to 'imagine the plight of non-readers who are still groping around the alphabet in a fog'.[6] The stories were of individuals, coping against the odds.

In Australia, one writer has suggested, such writing belonged to the 'language of advocacy', used by campaigning organisations pressing for funds, and describing the issue in terms that were largely 'individualist-welfarist'.[7] This was how some readers read my own writing of the time.[8] Brian Street, writing in 1990, refers to the prevalence at that time of 'Great Divide theory', according to which '"illiterates" are fundamentally separate from literates'.[9] Rereading the writings of the 1970s, I think something else was at work besides what he rightly sees as the false equation of illiteracy with

8

backwardness. I think both then and now, the issue also concerned the problem of representation. Those people with the 'specific insight into literacy' were not the people doing the work of reporting the experience of illiteracy; and those of us who were writing on their behalf were still learning to relate our own literacy 'needs' with those of other people.

The term 'literacy student', on the other hand, provides a different starting point for an educationalist writing about either literacy or illiteracy. With the change in teaching experience (from individual tuition to group) came the change in the the pictures in our heads. The people I recall now, in answering questions about 'illiteracy', are no longer single individuals speaking about their personal experiences. They are people actively participating in their own literacy education. The picture in the head is one of people talking to each other round a table, or clustered together in twos and threes, or, sometimes, silently, bent over paper and pen in the same room. The examples I choose to describe my perception of their progress will often be quotations from something they have said. The people I picture will, more often than not, be women.

This representation of literacy learning seems to me more useful than the earlier representations of the experience of illiteracy. Although some of this descriptive writing by educators may still be read as more pious than political, it is more honest. The effect is to emphasise not weaknesses but strengths. The evidence of learning is not that of texts mastered but of dialogue, discussion, questions. The description of the students is linked with their own (selected) accounts of what they are doing. Looking back over my own writing over the last fifteen years I notice it has been peppered with cameos and anecdotes of women and men, conversations and writings. ('It's Tuesday evening. It's raining. Seven people are in the room: four women, three men . . . ')[10] These pictures and stories were my effort to represent something of the testimony provided by those people themselves. There are more of them in the second part of this book.

It is of course true that 'literacy students' cannot be asked to be representative of the 'illiterate population' as a whole, any more than art students can be representative of the population of non-art students. Alan Charnley and Arthur Jones, writing in the late 1970s, called the literacy student 'one of a self-selected minority of a minority seeking to identify with values long rejected'.[11] On the national statistics of British illiteracy at the time, they point out that only 5 per cent were 'coming forward for tuition'. Their own study being based on interviews with only thirty-five such people (of whom sixteen were working as individuals with personal tutors), this may be read partially as a caution to themselves against the dangers of over-generalisation. Their own representation of the sample they met, however, is as 'the aristocrats of the educationally under-privileged, handicapped by lack of a particular skill, but unbowed'[12] – a phrasing which mixes the 'welfarist' with a vision of the heroically disabled, not altogether borne out by the words of the thirty-five people themselves.

AUTHORS AND INTERVIEWEES

In 1972, as a volunteer tutor and part-time paid organiser of one-to-one literacy teaching, I knew about the idea of 'confidence': literacy students then spoke of it, as the reward they had gained from hours, weeks and months of persistence with their own reading and writing with their individual tutors. Literacy is an everyday thing: it is the stuff of ordinary life, in the street, the post office, the kitchen. But the only literacy development by others on which a literacy teacher can report is that which she observes in a carefully staged situation: the literacy classroom. If someone in that room said that she had 'gained in confidence' since she began meeting her tutor six months before, that statement has to be recognised for what it is: a statement made in a specific context. Literacy organisers of the time knew we had to beware of making claims for that confidence gain being a life change. We often were not aware, and forgot to think about or imagine the other settings in which that same person may already be confident, far more confident than we; just as she, for the moment, had forgotten that other part of her life. Equally, we often forgot the possibility of generosity on the part of the speaker. Wishing to be generous to us, as tutors or literacy organisers, for what she saw as our generosity in taking her seriously, the literacy student gave us the compliment of attributing this change in herself to us – and to literacy itself.

Although forgetful, I was, like others, also aware that 'confidence' improvement alone was not enough to bring next year's grant in; and the measure I relied on then, in reporting the work of the hundreds of individuals who met with their individual tutors in the scheme I worked for, was a measure of reading; a score given on a test designed to assess the reading levels of children.

10

There are still literacy schemes today which use such tests. There is still a view that illiteracy is about individuals who – albeit through no fault of their own – failed these tests and others. There is still, in some places, an idea that literacy is all about reading. Until quite recently, the view that literacy education was mainly about men's education also prevailed. Fortunately, research and campaign work in the late 1980s meant that, by the time of International Literacy Year in 1990, it was no longer possible to hold a conference or publish a report without debating the equal rights of women to full literacy.[13]

Between 1975 and the late 1980s, however, much literacy work in this country focused on the job of persuading students to write, edit and publish writing about their own experience; including that of their own literacy education. In any writing I have published myself, these student publications have been without any doubt a richer source of material on which to draw than 'reading age' measures.[14] Indeed, I see such autobiographical texts by students as essential to any serious analysis of literacy work; precisely because they provide narratives over which the authors have control, as they rarely have over interviews they give. (The process of generating this writing is discussed further in chapter 5.)

These writings may, in many ways, be briefer and less eloquent than the author may be in speech; this would be true for most of us. Verbatim transcripts of interviews are undoubtedly full of unexpected revelations, diversions, and stories that an interested listener may encourage. But there are crucial limits to what is said in interview, which are different from those which operate for a new writer choosing their own words in writing, and which it is important to recognise in any attempt to use interview material as a means to 'represent' the experience of literacy students. In particular

(a) they are limited by what the interviewer is capable of seeing and hearing as we watch and listen to our interviewee; and

(b) the interviews represent only what any interviewee chooses to show of themselves, in that context, on that day, to that person.

In order to express some of the uses and meanings made of both illiteracy and literacy, then, we as writers have to be conscious of a use of literacy we are making ourselves: namely, our role as interpreters. We invent ways to persuade others to describe their experience, and then give our own interpretation to those descriptions, based on our own experience of literacy, and our own

11

purposes in attempting to represent that of others. The interviewer – interviewee pair is, if it is that of researcher–student, an inevitably unequal partnership. One, under persuasion, tells stories; the other listens, and later, selects from what she hears to tell others. (In Part II, chapter 3 I suggest other thinking on this relationship.) Less unequal is the interviewer–interviewee partnership in which both parties have a say, each listens, and both have some control over what is used from the interview later. When two or more people are in a position of exchanging tales from experience, in talk and later in writing, there is an increased opportunity for restating, redrafting, and retelling the tales with better accuracy (or more embellishments). In a group, with some common base of experience, there is the potential for different histories and learning experiences to be shared, explored and restated.

As writers and historians, literacy students writing about their experience also face problems of representation. But unlike the researcher or educator, they are representing their own experience; and some of the resulting accounts of the experience of 'illiteracy' have been somewhat different from the versions on which the 'campaign' of the 1970s had been based. Here is someone named simply as Gerry:

> I didn't feel ashamed that I couldn't read or write. In actual fact I regarded myself as being brilliant. I was a con man and I conned my own wife even. Mary didn't know I couldn't read or write until I told her one night when we went for a drink.[15]

Gerry and others, who have chosen to 'come out' – to reveal their position, join a literacy project and write about it – have suggested to the 'literate' campaigners such as me that our view of their experience was, quite simply, wrong – or at least, not by any means totally right.

Alan Charnley and Arthur Jones in their study of student learning in literacy, proposed a rather curious solution to the problem of representing a choice such as the one that Gerry made that night. They favoured seeing illiteracy and literacy in terms of a set of ideas about marginality. In their view, this concept helps, among other things, to explain the phenomenon of 'student drop out' at the start, or in the early stage of tuition. Rather than seeing the cause as poor or inappropriate teaching methods, they suggest, it could be seen as 'marginal' people preferring their marginality:

The common view is that the system has somehow failed them, but the theory of transformation from marginality suggests that this may not always be the reason. The marginal state has its advantages: it may be easier to go on 'passing' as one of a large group of sub-literates than to 'come out' with an acknowledgement of former marginality. The first step towards the centre may bring the nature of the change vividly to light and cause withdrawal as from a brink.[16]

While I find this unsatisfactory as a way of thinking about students' experience of teachers, it does raise an interesting question about people who, while finding reading and writing hard, never come near a literacy scheme in the first place, or decide to maintain their position as 'illiterate'. The question becomes, not 'what are we (education providers) doing wrong?' but 'why should the "illiterate" (or "sub-literate" as Charnley and Jones prefer to term them) see any advantages in "coming forward" for literacy teaching in any circumstances?'

There was, from what he tells us, a lot for Gerry to risk in 'coming out' to Mary. He describes his revelation and her reaction:

I'd built myself up with about five or six large whiskeys to tell her. I said, 'Mary, I'm illiterate'. She said, 'What?' She didn't believe me. She picked up a table mat and she said, 'You mean you couldn't even read that?'

The next few sentences suggest how much was entailed for him: how preferable his secrecy must have seemed; how dangerous the balancing act between his desire for honesty with her and his fear of her feelings at his deception.

I had to tell her because I felt awful dishonest. I knew everything about Mary, her background, her home, her life and I felt guilty that she didn't know this about me. It didn't feel clean to me.

This passage comes towards the end of an account by Gerry of his experience of schooling in rural Ireland, and his strategies for dealing with bureaucratic demands for literacy as an adult seeking work ('I'd say, "Never mind what it says on the paper, I want you to tell me of the conditions"'). It is interesting to apply the idea of marginality to the scene in the pub, as he recalls it. From a literate reader's reading of this passage, Gerry represents a position of the

13

illiterate's courage, both in his deception and in his revelation: and the literacy educator's work is vindicated by his accolade for the literacy classes he is now attending; 'they built up my confidence', he writes, 'it's like gradually waking up after a long sleep'.

But we are still left with another question. In the passage quoted, Gerry said, quite categorically, that far from feeling ashamed of his illiteracy, he had regarded himself as brilliant. This is a statement that is easy to overlook, in a piece which earlier describes not this pride, but a sense of shame and embarrassment in his illiteracy (and for which the editors have picked out this aspect as the title). Nevertheless, this statement is there; and the question it raises is this: what exactly was the difference between the sense of pride and confidence Gerry reports before he revealed his illiteracy, and the confidence he says he 'built up' after joining a group of others in order to become literate?

DESCRIBE OR QUANTIFY?

Achievements in pride and confidence, meanwhile, do not easily fit into quantifiable accounts of literacy development. The problem of representation for the educator who has convened these groups as classes, part of overall 'provision', is this: how do we represent to others – people who are unfamiliar with that room and those people, talking round a table, clustered together, and writing – just what it is that we have seen and heard? For that matter, should we even make the attempt? There is a view (which I sometimes share) that the proper authors for this representation work are not the teachers but the students, and that one day the movement of student publishing in adult literacy will grow into a gigantic literature of learning autobiographies, which will make redundant any further need for teachers to explain, describe and evaluate.

However, there remain two reasons for literacy teachers ourselves to struggle with the issue of writing about our work. The first concerns ourselves as writers, and amounts to this: we, too, are entitled to reflect on experience. (We have, week after week, year after year, countless experiences of our own and other people's literacy development to make sense of.) The second is the harsh pragmatics of our job: unless we insist on arguing for and explaining a particular position about literacy, the funding and status of the work sinks back into the furthest margins of public policy from where it began.

Some years ago writing about the problem of writing research reports, I asked: 'Is this a letter, or is it news that we are writing? Is it a detective novel, or a piece of our autobiography?' I was trying to suggest alternative means of expressing the findings of research studies to the classical ones (aim–method–findings–conclusion).[17] Six months later I found myself facing a committee of the college where I work, in which the work of the Lee Centre was being reviewed. I have been haunted ever since by the question one of the committee asked me that morning, and by my fumbled efforts to answer it. 'So what are your outcomes?' he asked. I began to answer him, by telling him a story of a woman who had come to one of our literacy classes, and subsequently joined the 'return to study' course for women at the Centre we called 'New Horizons'. 'No, no,' he interrupted, impatiently, 'I'm not asking for stories: I want to know the outcomes – how many of your students become literate?' Eight committee members were sitting there waiting, with him, for my answer. Hurt, confused and angry, I mumbled a figure, which I said (in my anxiety for truth) was approximate. The chair of the committee reproved me for not having more exact statistics.

Ever since that day in that meeting, I have looked with different eyes on the statistical graphs of other organisations, the figures of success and achievement, and resolved to deal differently with truth. I have many times replayed the same scene, with the same question, and given a different reply. The answer to the question must be: all who come as literacy students achieve literacy. All of them, in truth, bring literacy experience to the classroom. All take with them literacy experience when they leave. This is, like any claim to success, both true and untrue.

Research reports which offer quantity results are comforting. Reading-age leaps are reassuring. The teacher can show she is delivering the goods; authorities can see evidence of money well spent. But the picture that made me hesitant to give the comforting answer, the answer that would (perhaps) have altered the balance of an academic committee's view of the worth of a literacy project, was the picture of another room, with other people: that room of people, talking, listening, writing, doubting and questioning. I sat in this committee on their behalf; I wanted to convey their intellectual and creative energy, not reduce them to passive statistical puppets. I did not want to betray them.

This is not liberal sentimentality. The determined effort to represent and describe how and in what way a number of individuals in a room express their knowledge and their learning is a much harder discipline than that of giving them tests, adding up scores, and fixing the figures.

AUTHENTIC VOICES

'Illiterate', I suggested earlier, is a social category: 'adult literacy student' an educational one. What is the reality of someone's decision to move from one position to another? And when are these the categories that the person would choose for themselves?

A number of literacy campaigns have taken the banner of a 'fight against illiteracy', in response to a perceived 'crisis', as a rescue operation for victims of a distressing condition. Jean-Paul Hautecoeur, a writer and researcher on literacy work in Canada, has argued that this crusading approach has led to an unexpected problem. In Quebec, he reports, there is a greater supply of literacy provision than demand for it, and asks the question: 'Why are learners not coming forward?' He summarises the answers proposed so far under five headings:

1 The problem is exaggerated. The definition of illiteracy should be narrowed down again to the literal or strict sense of the word.
2 Resources for preliteracy are insufficient. The move towards a 'new management model' of literacy education has excluded resources for outreach, and needs returning to community action.
3 Services are inadequate. The move towards 'academic upgrading' has denied other uses for literacy: the most effective recruiters to literacy would be literacy students themselves, with other insights into literacy interests.
4 Illiteracy causes people to hide. Literacy services should have been kept to the original one-to-one approach; but this view, he suggests, has perpetuated the very stigma it intends to combat.
5 Perceptions of the problem are outdated. This, he comments, is the dominant view in currency: more businesslike and technological approaches need addressing to serve literacy 'in the world of work'.

Hautecoeur finds all these answers leave out the crucial one: namely, that the 'need' for literacy has been argued as a result of 'outside pressure', and that:

16

Illiteracy is first and foremost a definition formulated by the cultured or moderately educated classes. The division of society along this sociolinguistic line is a middle-class perception. *But, while the division is very real and recognised by the poorer classes, it does not necessarily lead to literacy training* [my italics].

His conclusion is that there are only two possible courses of action: to use marketing strategies to 'up the demand', or to 'return to grass roots and determine optimum conditions for the joint development . . . of the supply of services and demand'.[18]

Back in 1975, in the UK, I and others were using the term 'illiterate' without recognising our class position in Hautecoeur's terms – precisely in order to challenge what we saw as 'other people's' oppressive attitudes. Two letters I wrote which were published in the press that year illustrate this. In the first, I was answering what I saw to be a sensationalist and patronising view of illiteracy expressed in a feature from the previous week's issue of a newspaper:

Illiterates are not born, they are made. Certainly, they need help – most of them in recognising that they are perfectly adequate human beings. In his article 'Words that are worth £1 million', H.J. Pankhurst has a condescending view of their targets. Does a woman with reading difficulties really only aspire to cook more imaginatively? He was nearer the real issue when he described Mary Smith as a 'wow at work, but won't socialise . . . '

When the rest of the world has been telling you that you are backward, stupid, lazy or even culturally deprived, your willingness to 'socialise' is bound to be small.[19]

The use of the inverted commas in the second letter suggests I have some small hesitations about the word: but no hesitation, it seems, in saying how people in this category feel:

Too many 'illiterate' or 'semi-literate' adults are so profoundly cast down in their own estimation that they not only disbelieve the possibility that they can learn to read and spell adequately; they disbelieve that they have anything of interest to say, let alone write, that anyone else would want to listen to or read. Yet we know, once people are strengthened in self-

17

confidence and ability, that everyone is capable of writing something worth reading. Often, at the simple reading level, there is nothing else of adult interest that *is* worth reading.[20]

The 'Right to Read' campaign document, also published in 1974, used the term 'adult illiterate' five times in a couple of pages: focusing as it did on a group of people, a social category, for whom public attention and resources should be allocated.[21] Other writers, in the same year, discussed the legitimate needs of this group in the same terms.[22] One, at least, was raising then the important question, 'What concept of literacy is held by those who plan projects?'[23] – a question which he suggested was encouraged by the growing debate about literacy in schools, prompted by the publication of the 1975 Bullock Report, 'A language for life'.

Meanwhile, at an international level, these problems and questions were being addressed rather differently. The UNESCO Experimental World Literacy Programme was under review. At the now famous 'Persepolis Conference' there was energetic criticism of a view of literacy and illiteracy on which it had been founded. The conference called for what we might now see to be an alliance with, rather than an aid mentality towards, the illiterate. 'Greater respect' was urged for what the people concerned already knew, and more consultation with them, instead of obedience to 'bureaucratic decisions imposed from outside and above'. It declared: 'The motivation of those involved will be stronger if each community is itself given the opportunity of carrying out the literacy project'.[24]

Most of this chapter has suggested that third-person accounts of illiterates are a thing of the past. This does not altogether appear to be so. Promotional material for International Literacy Year included a variety of images and representations of adult interests in literacy which suggested that the idea of 'the illiterate as other people' persists. The problem with this, as I have tried to suggest, is that it gives permission to the reporters on illiteracy to tell us their version of the people they describe, without apparent need to substantiate their description. *Looking for words* was a film made for International Literacy Year in this country, with the purpose of promoting the importance of adult literacy – particularly as a means to employment. This is the reporter's comment on one of these people, named, in the film, as Parmena: 'She is the kind of person who naturally fitted into work in a hospital. For many years it was enough. It was satisfying to serve.'[25]

The voice of the reporter (a man) is heard as we watch Parmena pouring tea for patients. Parmena, as it happens, is black. The film makers doubtless intended this description of her to be warm and positive. Nevertheless, the wording of the reporter strikes a shocking note. Most viewers, if they stop and think, are aware that hospital auxiliaries are low-paid, that the health service is under-staffed, and that black women have long experience of low-paid work. Other factors than a feeling of satisfaction with serving others could be suggested for Parmena's remaining in her particular job. This comment by the authors of a study of black women's experience in this country, themselves black women, suggest what these factors could be:

For many Black women who joined the NHS with the intention of becoming nurses, this was to remain an elusive goal. Relegated to the hospitals' kitchens and laundries, or trudging the wards as tea-ladies, cleaners and orderlies, we were to have firsthand experience of the damning assumptions which define our role here. The patients saw it as fitting that we should be doing Britain's dirty work and often treated us with contempt.[26]

The problem which the film-makers gave themselves is this: they took it upon themselves to represent what 'kind of person' Parmena was. With experience of hospital work confined, perhaps, to occasionally that of being a patient, they had their own certainties about what she was 'naturally fitted' to be or do. This left them open to being seen, by viewers, as racist: for the work this woman was doing is notoriously low-paid and low-status, and the woman is black. (Had they suggested she was 'naturally fitted' to being a film director, rather than a hospital worker, the statement might have had a different effect.)

In summary, third-person representation of 'illiterates as other people' always runs the risk of stereotyping, and is inadequate, by itself, to describe the decisions and contexts implied by any individual or group taking steps to claim education for themselves. For a fuller understanding of the attitudes and social experience both of illiteracy and literacy, we need, instead, authentic voices, speaking from their own experience, on their own terms. The means by which these voices may be found and heard include: the gathering of student experience in class discussion, the practice of student conferences, and the exchange made possible by published

19

writing and broadcast programmes. Authentic representation depends as much on who is making the statement as on what they are saying. (Who holds the camera, microphone, or pen? and who decides what will be edited out?)

We live in a culture in which the dominant media are owned by large conglomerates, and our opinions and ideas are formed by versions of reality which are controlled and limited. My own persistent optimism in the possibility and the power of authentic voices being heard derives from an experience of literacy work which develops alternative media.

One voice speaks; another answers. Across the space of distance and time, a single woman's account of her fears in dealing with literacy, published in an early issue of the national literacy paper, *Write First Time*, spoke to countless other people who recognised their own experience in hers. Distributed regularly for ten years to literacy centres across the UK, the paper attracted a wide readership; and letters from readers, themselves literacy students, gave some idea of their reactions. This one appeared in response to the article on 'fear' (the emphasis in the last line is mine):

Dear Write First Time
I read your article about the lady who was frightened at filling forms in for a job. I know how she feels because it's happened to me many times. I've gone for a job and it's been a job I've liked but when they show me the forms I've just walked out, saying, "I'll think about it and let you know". I've lost some really nice jobs over it. *Now I think I'm silly for not telling them.*
Yours,
Linda.[27]

This letter not only tells us about Linda's experience of 'illiteracy', it also tells us about a change in her own sense of identity. She no longer felt alone. It's a short step for her to decide she will 'tell them'; and from 'telling them' to losing her fear of 'their' power to put her down.

Such a change could also have come about through the experience of being part of a regular literacy group, as another writer, Susan White reports. In the same publication in which the passage by Gerry appeared, she writes, first, about her memories of school, and of the child psychologist describing her as 'backward'. Then she tells how she felt 'a fool' when, as an adult, she first joined a basic education course. Then she describes her sense of change in those versions of herself as she got to know the other people in the group and her place within it:

> Many times I felt, 'I can't go up to their standard', but you see my problem was only really small compared to the others . . . It doesn't only help you to read and write and get through your problems, but it helps you in other ways as well. It helps you to express yourself and it helps you for new ideas . . . It's not like being in a school *it's more like being in a group*, like in a family. They don't push you like they do at school. The atmosphere is very important. You've got to feel as if you're equal. You mustn't feel as if you can sense hostility 'cause . . . you'll go straight back again . . . I used to hide it, but not now 'cause I'm not ashamed of it any more. *I know there's a lot of people who are like me.*[28] [my italics].

In this short passage Susan White speaks, as Virginia McLean and John Paul did earlier, about a move from individual to collective identity. The course she attended was known as the TSD Preparatory Course. These courses, first funded by the Manpower Services Commission in the same year that the Write First Time project began (1975) were the only full-time courses in basic education that ever existed in this country (outside the Army). Initially they ran on a forty-eight-week year; by 1977 there were 1,544 trainees nationally who attended such courses; from 1980 they began to be cut; and by 1985 they ended altogether. A remarkable video film made by eight students from the last Brighton Preparatory Course was shown to a large public audience in 1986 as part of a campaign to prevent the ending of this and other courses. The film-makers had interviewed ex-students and their colleagues about the course experience, and set this in the economic context of unemployment and educational cuts.

Such a film costs time to make. For any group to take on the task of collecting and interpreting the experience of a larger group is a huge undertaking. In representing the experience of illiteracy and literacy, the medium of writing is still at the heart of all media representations. And writing, representing experience expressively and coherently, with the full stops in the right place and no misspellings to trip up the reader, takes a lot of time. In her research on literacy students' experience in Hackney, Julia Clarke says her original intention was to involve students in conducting interviews.

She reports an unexpected difficulty, which so slowed up the process that, because of her own time constraints, she had to drop this idea. The students being interviewed wanted to help their interviewers.[29] The interviewers (literacy students themselves), concerned to write what they told them, were also concerned to get the writing spelt correctly and in 'proper sentences'.

2

THE TRUTH FOR NOW

A tutor suggested that I visit Lucille, who had started at [the centre] with very limited literacy skills and had progressed to a college course. However, when I went to see Lucille, she told me that she had attended [a class] many years ago, before starting at [the centre] and that even then she had already been able to fill in forms and read letters. She had completed her schooling in the West Indies and felt insulted at the suggestion that she had not learnt to read and write at school. Lucille said she began to attend classes because her reading was not as fluent as she had wanted and her spelling was 'not that good'.[1]

Who was telling the truth? Who knew most about 'the truth' being talked about? As the last chapter suggested, representing other people's truths is a precarious business. In this, I pursue the issue of representation in describing our own experience. The tutor talking to the researcher was describing not her own, but a (sincerely held) perception of Lucille's abilities and history in literacy education. Lucille's perception of the same experience was different. Had the tutor not known that she had already been able to 'fill in forms and read letters'? Or was this what she meant by 'very limited literacy skills'? Truth concerns both facts and their significance. In this account, the tutor had apparently got her facts wrong in reporting Lucille's school literacy; she also appeared to give a different significance to what Lucille was able to do in reading and writing as an adult.

Writing about our own experience, as I am partly doing in this book, means both reporting 'facts' (thinking, by ourselves or with other people, at a particular moment in time) and attributing significance to them. In this chapter I discuss first the relationship between 'truths for teachers' and 'truths for students' and the different expectations of both as writers. The next three sections discuss three areas closely related to each other in any writing: 'truth or fiction?', 'truth and talk' and 'truth and style'.

TRUTHS FOR TEACHERS, TRUTHS FOR STUDENTS

In recent years much energy in adult and further education has been given to finding ways of awarding credit to students' learning and progress. It is common to hear discussions of 'building', or 'constructing' portfolios of work as a means to this end. I take this to mean persuading students to collect and keep their writing (or artwork) in some sort of order, in order to be able to present it as evidence, at a later date, to a prospective course tutor or employer. The movement to 'accredit prior learning' is an important one.[2] Many people with a history of low-paid part-time irregular employment, particularly women with years of putting other people's care before their own, are not in the habit of declaring or analysing this history with the purpose of presenting it as an account of publicly recognisable achievements; for the very good reason that they have heard too many other people dismissing such experience as unimportant.[3] So it is an enormous and vital part of any literacy education to persuade students to persist with the effort of making statements about their lives and learning.

The metaphor of construction is not one that comes easily to me, however. Perhaps because I am female, and more skilled in other crafts than those of building, I am more comfortable, in talking about writing, with words to do with spinning yarn, following threads, knitting themes together, and embroidering details. Rather than 'building' writing about experience, then, I (and maybe you) prefer the image of weaving strands together – a mix of warp and weft which leads to patterns emerging which are never entirely predictable.

James Britton, who for six years directed the British Schools Council Research Project into Development of Writing Ability in Children (age 11–18), has been a source of much wisdom on the subject of expressive writing. He distinguished between writing to get something done (which he called transactional writing) and writing to reflect and interpret experience (which he called poetic writing).[4] Interestingly, the move to teach writing in order to accredit prior learning is a move to try and give poetic writing a transactional function. For Britton, learning from experience is 'the most fundamental and universal kind of learning for human beings'; to do this learning means 'bringing our past to bear upon the present'.[5] In talking about experience, we add to and change what we say about it in the light of what others say in response: so one kind of truth meets another, and makes new patterns.

What we may have learned from our life history, to some extent determines how we choose to write about it. If I say 'I put on a tape of Ella Fitzgerald when I wrote that paragraph', it's a statement of history; but it also implies that I have learned that her singing gives me a certain kind of pleasure that might help me write. If I say, 'in my experience, listening to Ella Fitzgerald singing helps me write better', it's a statement of learning – but it implies a history of doing this several times, as a habit. If I was talking to you about it, you might say that for you, listening to Bruch's Violin Concerto No. 1 in G minor or the Bolivian folk group Rumillajta works better when you want to write; which will remind me that sometimes that is true for me, as well. (Meanwhile, the last three paragraphs have changed from one draft to another as I made a decision, late in the writing, to weave into my fabric a short thread from some of James Britton's work, of which you will find another strand towards the end of this chapter.)

It is a commonplace for literacy educators to cite their students' reports of increases in confidence as a benefit which they gain from their classroom experience.[6] At the same time, it has been a commonplace in sociological and historical research to qualify the firsthand testimony of individuals as 'subjective' and only partial truth.[7] Evidence of immediate participants in a particular historical moment must be substantiated with other, official and public sources if 'the truth' about a period or an event is to be adequately established. Reminiscence work, in more recent years, has been hailed both as valuable therapy for the participants and as dubious history.[8] Students are encouraged to engage in experiential writing, to write for themselves of their own learning; in so doing, they are using language for purposes that are both poetic (by its nature subjective) and transactional (intending to make a persuasive case as to the value of that experience). Literacy education which involves accreditation means, in short, challenging the usual separation of subjective and objective truths: generating personal and reflective writing with the aim of asserting that these personal reflections have worth in terms of impersonal criteria.

Teachers of this writing, however, have been schooled in academic literacy; and in our own public writing, there are constant doubts as to what exactly should be the mix of personal and impersonal.

My own history of learning and theorising about literacy, like that of any other literacy educator, is subject to feeling and emotion. My 'portfolio' of private and published writing over twenty years, as I suggested in the previous chapter, is the result of what, at the time, I felt capable of saying. Sometimes the feelings it conveys are anger; sometimes joy. Much is omitted. Other life-events belonging to my personal history are, usually, selected out. They belong, so my thinking goes, to a different portfolio. Yet any teacher brings, as students do, a certain amount of emotional luggage into the classroom. The influence of other political, social and economic realities touches all of us in different ways. But we see our purpose, both in the class time and in our published writing, as that of providing conditions for the achievement of our students' purposes: namely, to improve their reading and writing abilities. So we keep our secrets: our own political or moral positions and personal lives are only drawn into the work under certain conditions, or are left to be glimpsed through our 'professional' texts.[9]

The tension, for literacy educators, is between the subjective writing we believe in for our students and the culture of a different kind of writing expected of us in our professional roles. Nor are we always, as writers in this culture, clear as to the exact nature of these expectations. In a fascinating study of 'literacy in the university', Brigid Ballard and John Clanchy carried out a detailed analysis of lecturers' comments on their students' essays. In the academic world, they suggest, the newcomer has to 'crack the code' and learn a literacy that has its own rules and meanings:

The first steps towards cultural literacy in the university are the same as those that apply in any other literate culture. You must first crack the basic code, begin to master the alphabet of linguistic and cognitive behaviour. The letter 'A' for example, introduces key elements in the academic culture, as well as standing for 'Excellent' at the end of an essay. 'A', the new student learns, stands for *Analysis* ('I want analysis – not mere description'). 'A' also stands for *Argument* ('I want an argument, not a polemic'. 'This is mere opinion – where is your argument?') 'A' stands for *Assertion* ('What is the evidence for this claim? You can't just assert something . . . ') And for *Assumption* . . . [10]

'We are all', these writers conclude, 'more or less literate in different contexts of culture at different stages of our development'. (In chapter 7 I return to some of these different literacies with a comparison of two groups' reactions to the same literacy task.) Mere description, mere opinion and mere assertions are not the stuff of academic literacy. They are, however, the bread and butter of writing curricula vitae – those pieces of writing so essential to an individual's chances of gaining certain jobs; the texts which are the daily fare of basic education and job skills courses; the kind of writing which presents an 'authorised version' of our auto-biography.

There is, then, an imbalance between the truths we ask of students in adult education and those once asked of us, in our own histories as students, and still inside our heads when we ourselves write. (As I suggest towards the end of this chapter, this sometimes results in teachers setting limits on the style in which their students undertake the autobiographical writing we encourage them to do.) In direct opposition to the academic world's hostility to description, opinion and assertion is the logic of experiential learning and adult literacy practice, which goes like this:

1 Experience is worthy of recording.
2 In order to recognise our learning history – mistakes and achieve-ments, influences and inspirations – we have to re-examine this experience in its context.
3 Writing is a means of doing this reflection, analysis and new thinking, and of presenting the result to others to whom we want to present our experience as worthy.

To mark the learning means to mark the moments of change. In a very practical sense, this means that writing always needs naming and dating, and it means taking responsibility, with the use of the personal pronoun, for that learning.[11] (My history of music and writing – if I was to write such a thing – would be incomplete if I did not add to one of the sentences above that the time when I first noticed Ella Fitzgerald's music was helpful to me was late on a Wednesday afternoon in August 1991.) Making 'portfolios' means making visible some movement and development; both assume having work to compare with at some earlier time. The process invites a student to be her own historian.

TRUTH OR FICTION?

'I can't think what to write.' 'I can't spell.' Is there so much difference between these two? At every word, sentence or page all writers struggle, in different ways, with the question 'Is this true?' As readers, we may have that question further back in our minds; the authority of the finished text is between us. The job of teachers is often to do one thing with writing and the other with reading. We ask students to stop, reread and question what they are reading (Do you like it? Do you agree with it? Why? Why not?) Then we ask them to write. Just write, we say. Don't worry about the spelling; just get something down.

But asking anyone to 'just write,' some researchers have acknowledged, is a tall order. Writing is something we do a great deal less than reading. Gunther Kress, in his study of young children's writing development, has even asserted that 'there are a large number of people, the majority in any society, who never or hardly ever write'. This is partly, he argues, to do with fundamental differences, often ignored or misunderstood, between speech and writing. For too long, in Kress's view, there has been a false idea that writing is no more than speech plus 'mechanics and conventions'. Instead, he says, one key characteristic of written language marks it out from spoken language: writing (or prose writing, at least) requires sentences. Producing sentences means planning the order and relative weight of what we have to say. Speech, by contrast, with an audience which is visible to the speaker, can assume some shared knowledge, is more usually a series of 'chains', and has the help of intonation, gesture and facial expression to support it. Rather than saying that learning to write is like learning to put speech on paper, Kress argues, it is far more useful, and more accurate, to describe it as *learning a second language*.[12]

My argument here is that, since getting writing started is undeniably hard, the idea of 'the truth for now' is worth exploring. It means saying: this is not the final statement that you could make, nor the total truth that everyone would agree with – it's the truth for now, for you. Next week you'd write the same thing differently. Six years ago, the writing you did about it gave an entirely other angle on it. For now, this is what has come to your mind.

If it is useful in persuading ourselves to start writing, I believe 'the truth for now' idea is also an important one to hold on to in assessing what we read of other writers. If we keep it in mind, then we make conscious at one and the same time both our own contexts as readers and the particular historical circumstances of the writing. Here are two examples.

The first is a text written from the experience of Aymaran women in Bolivia. The text, a reading primer called *We Are Able* was used in a women's education programme in Bolivia in 1984. The words originate from 'participative investigation' with fifty-six women's education groups, with themes chosen by the women themselves and photographs taken by them of each other. The 'truths' of the text include sentences such as these:

I am a person and nobody has the right to knock me down . . .
In my family everyone gives something . . .
To participate is to change our lives . . .
If we work together with the community council we will advance . . .
We want a free and just Bolivia.[13]

The most attractive way of relating our life as readers with that of ourselves as writers I find to be Paulo Freire's invitation to get inside the head of the writer when we read. In discussing 'the act of study', he tells us to read as if we were the writer:

It's impossible to study seriously if the reader faces a text as though magnetized by the author's word, mesmerized by a magical force . . . Seriously studying a text calls for an analysis of the study of the one who, through studying, wrote it.[14]

For that group of women in that particular time, in the particular set of conditions, in that particular place, those sentences were the truths of their lives. As a white European woman, sitting where I am with the book in my hand, I wonder 'were they true for all the women? are they still true?' As a reader from another country, another time, I can take a cynic's reading and regard these statements as empty slogans; or, taking account of the genesis of the writing, I can respect their conviction and recognise that, if some of the sentences read to me as slogans, it may be because of the limits of my own culture. Who am I to disbelieve a woman who says 'In my family everyone gives something' or a group which declares 'We want a free and just Bolivia'? One answer is: someone who, in order adequately to study this text, still needs an analysis of those who, 'through studying, wrote it'.

The second is an extract from an interview transcript in a 'bestselling' book about dyslexia:

> I see totally visually. I don't see in words, and words still stay visual with me. The most wonderful thing in my childhood was the Coca-Cola sign in Piccadilly, to me it was the greatest work of art I had ever seen. The lights at Piccadilly Circus were just poetry. And the minute I could read, all that went, which was very sad.[15]

The person speaking is someone named as Sally, a theatre designer. She is speaking in interview to Susan Hampshire, author of an earlier book describing her own struggles with dyslexia. The truth of Sally and the thirty or so other interviewees in this book could be said to be that they were talking, with a sense of equality, to someone who had experienced (and had said in public that she had experienced) humiliations and frustrations of illiteracy similar to their own. My caution, in reading this collection, is in the declared purpose of the book, and hence the emphasis of the editing. Its subtitle is 'Winning in life despite dyslexia'. Susan Hampshire's purpose is to show how public and individual success is possible – even though you cannot read and write. Her interviewees include business men, television producers, actresses, athletes, judges, architects and politicians.

All these have truths for themselves; and the interviews refer to a range of feelings and experiences. The book has been put together with a message: you can win, too. However, there is an odd omission. Susan Hampshire describes how 'heart-breaking' it is to know that there are 'over two million dyslexics in the United Kingdom', which suggests a use of the campaign figures of the 1975 adult literacy campaign. But, while a list of organisations offering diagnosis and remedial treatment for dyslexics appears at the end, with encouragement to anxious parents to seek advice from them for any child displaying reading and writing difficulties, no reference is made to any educational opportunities for adults.

Sally's 'truth' in this extract is interesting. Most of us, of course, do see 'totally visually', unless we have sight impairment. However, her view of literacy's disadvantages is unusual: that the 'poetry' of words in lights was gone once she could read them. She had 'won', but there was something that, in the process, she had also lost.

TRUTH AND TALK

Edited transcripts of talk are by their nature only partial truths. We have no knowledge of Susan Hampshire's own prompts and comments in that or other interviews. However, we may guess that there was some sense of sympathy between interviewer and inter- viewee, with a culture and educational background in common. The next two examples suggest how people in interview arrange- ments on this equal footing can inspire each other to recreate new or forgotten truths.

The park and the bubble gum

One Friday morning in 1988 in South London, I invited a group of women to talk about colours. The group knew each other well. I had joined them for three writing workshops in the twelfth week of their twenty-week course. From a box of wax crayons, I asked them to choose, on impulse, the colour they wanted at that moment. Then I asked them to talk to a partner about their colour, what it made them think of, and why they liked it. I explained the purpose of the work would be to get some ideas going for them to use in drafting a piece of writing. The partner was to act as secretary for the speaker and note down some of what she said. After comparing notes in the group, speakers would then use the notes made by their secretaries to develop a piece of prose – going from the odd words and phrases in the notes to sentences and stories.

These were the two stages of work by a couple of writers in the group. First, the lists with the secretary:

Green (Cheryl writing for Lucy)
grass, trees
all things that are living
parks, countryside
park on a summer's day when I was little
Ireland
my younger brother in the park

Pink (Marjorie writing for Liz)
bubble gum

31

spring and summer blossom
pleasant things
scents in the garden
pink garden

Lucy, thinking about her 'park on a summer's day when I was little', went on to write this:

> I can remember when I was about eight years old, taking my younger brother to the park in the afternoon. I would take my big red scooter and he would hold on tightly to his ball. They were always bright warm summer days, and the park was always crowded with lots of people.

Liz, recalling a story about bubble gum, wrote this:

> I was six or seven years old. I lived in a block of flats. There was a large gang of children. I was the youngest – we always did what the older ones said.
>
> One day my brother and his friend from next door were playing on the steps. A boy we nick-named 'four eyes' would ride through our estate as a short cut from the sweet shop to his house. We didn't like this; he was on our 'Patch'. We knocked him off his bicycle and stole his bubble gums.
>
> I felt a sense of power, because it was the first time I had ever bullied someone, and it worked. I expected him to 'beat me up'. I also felt guilty and cruel.

For the women, these recollected moments belonged to particular places and times. In addition, the Friday morning on which they wrote about them would itself be the subject for later recollection. The dates on those pieces of writing allow them at a later time also to recall the conversation, as well as to compare these writings with later work – a comparison not only with any 'progress' in their technical literacy (spelling, punctuation and so on), but also with any differences between the life they were living that week and the life they lived when they came to reread this. For sure, the same colour, explored on another occasion, talked about with other people, with a different mood, would almost certainly suggest other associations to them. Those differences would be to do with all sorts of other changes in their own lives and the world they are living in.

Penny peas and star apple

The issue of 'the truth', then, is one of history and context. The delight of reminiscence groups, as two of us suggested a few years ago[16] is precisely the possibility of 'redrafting the truth'. It is the possibility which James Britton described, of representation 'as a cumulative process'.[17] A group of older people meet, not in the name of literacy, but of history, to recall and recreate their memories. Some of this recollection may be taped or noted; when they meet the following week, they can amend or add to this record. Disagreements over names, dates and places can be reflected on and changed. If no one is feeling on trial for 'the whole truth and nothing but the truth', the art of story-telling can be given full rein. Here is an example of the process of talk in which some common knowledge can link to, check and compare with different recollections:

> Five women, representing between them five different Caribbean islands, discuss different names and uses of plants and different kinds of spiritualism recalled from their childhood in the Caribbean . . . Three of them compare the names they recall for a plant that one, from Trinidad, calls *penny peas* (yellow blossom, with a green pod); another, from Guyana, asks if she recalls *star apple*. They agree that *balata*, which grows very high, is lovely. A third, also from Trinidad, tries to recall a plant she thinks is called *cocoreet* – or is it *pewa?* The conversation slows, then speeds up again, as the others pick up, in their minds, the picture she paints of it:
>
> T: I know what you – pewa.
> B: Pewa. And they grow on high trees and –
> T: – yes. And as you say that, I can remember seeing the big bunches of pewa falling on the floor, you know. Pewa. Some people call it peeleewa.
> B: That's right, yes. And chataigne, too. I love chataigne. I used to love chataigne soup.
> T: It's similar to chestnut, you know . . . [18]

Truth needs listening for. Listening is a key to much literacy use in more formal situations. (I'm thinking particularly of the problem, discussed in the last chapter of this book, of taking minutes of a meeting.) The listening that is going on here has as its purpose not the correction of mistakes, but the increase of knowledge. Each time

I read this extract from the transcript talk, it reads like a piece of music: one voice chiming in and adding to what the other has said, adding and elaborating. Not all reminiscence talk in a group contains the sense of agreement which this extract conveys; and not all members of any such group may share a willingness to contribute either their memories or their reflections on those memories in the way this group does. It happens that the subject, in this group, is one which evokes a pleasure in the tastes and names of the fruit they are discussing. Truth, in this conversation, is not being claimed by one speaker over another. No-one is suggesting that there is only one right answer to the name of the fruit. In that sense, none of the speakers are being silenced.

TRUTH AND STYLE

There are, in our language, several different ways of saying the same thing. Talk between friends is talk with listeners who are present. In writing, the reader is absent. For a writer to believe there is a real choice open to her of *how* she writes, she also has to believe, first in her own purpose in writing and, second, in the reality of an interested reader. In 'Learning from Experience' I offered an exercise to try out different styles of making the same statement with different purposes in mind. The example I gave was this sentence: (i) 'Her car is a white Morris 1100 which can drive at a speed of up to 70 mph'. I suggested two other ways of conveying this information: one aiming to create a positive effect: (ii) 'She is the lucky owner of a gleaming white Morris 1100 which cruises at 70 mph'; and the other, expressing the opposite; (ii) 'Her car is a dirty old Morris banger which reaches 70 on a good day.'

Sentence (i) is an apparently unadorned statement of fact. The writer is not setting out to persuade her reader; she is not revealing, either, any opinion of her own on the subject. In sentence (ii) the use of the adjectives 'lucky' and 'gleaming' imply favourable feelings which the writer has, and which she wants her reader to share. ('Cruises' has a pleasurable association, too; unlike the plain 'drive'.) The last sentence, by contrast, is disparaging. This car is a waste of money.

Different truths are at work with different choices of vocabulary; but for many student writers, there are at least four difficulties in the way of their making a choice. First, there is the sense that there is a proper way to write, which other people know but which is out of their reach. Second, they are well aware that in a number of writing situations, personal feeling is out of bounds to the writer – and they are unsure which those situations are. Third, in more personal writing, they are uncertain about how much their reader actually wants to read what they may want to say. And last but not least, they are permanently hedged in with a sense that their technical writing abilities are wanting – that their handwriting, spelling and punctuation will be ridiculed by their reader. I will briefly discuss each of these difficulties. First, the issue of status and writing.

Government and academic organisations alike have had reason to pause, in recent years, and question both their conventions and their myths about writing. The 'right to have things readably written'[19] has been argued for energetically since 1979, when the Plain English Campaign was launched.[20] Chrissie Maher, before co-founding the campaign, worked as a community worker in Salford, helping people to fill in forms. Since then, she and the Campaign have been helping form-writers to make their forms more readable for people to fill in, and taking on commissions to rewrite and redesign documents intended for public circulation. The campaign against 'gobbledygook' has, she reports, sometimes been an uphill struggle. People who are used to seeing long texts as the result of clever thinking and hard work, do not find it easy to recognise simplicity in writing as, sometimes, still harder work. Short reports can be, Chrissie Maher argues, more effective to their purpose than longer ones; but, for this to be accepted, it means:

> trying to impress on chief executives and heads of departments that if they're given two sides of A4 as an accumulation of four to six weeks work they shouldn't be appalled or think their employee has been running around shopping instead of working. They've been struggling, cutting down, re-wording.[21]

Others have taken up the problems of 'organisational literacy' and offered analyses of how information can be made more accessible.[22] The move in teaching practice encouraged by the Plain English Campaign is the move from teaching students skills in completing forms, towards an approach which invites them to rewrite them or even create new ones.

The second problem I have mentioned is the relationship between personal and impersonal writing. Here, to illustrate this, are two different versions of the kind of text which belongs in the area of 'statusful writing': the introduction to an academic research report. The first example runs as follows:

> This report offers an analysis of the factors contributing to perceived inequalities in educational achievement, and attempts to suggest some causes for failure in a particular group. By means of a comparative study, collating data from two discrete samples, it has been found that these causes may be attributed to uneven distribution of access to opportunity.

All fairly impressive – and all entirely noncommittal. We have no idea of the author's identity or view of the conclusions. The only agent in either sentence is 'the report'. The second example is an alternative version, written with other intentions:

> In this report I say that we live in a class society. I say that the kids who did well at school, who spoke the same language as and got the approval of the teacher, go on getting the approval of other teachers – called lecturers. I say that the kids who felt bad in classrooms are made to feel it's their fault, not anyone else's, and that, when they grow up, they can't make it because they are thought to have the wrong bits of mental equipment. I say all this on the basis of research with two different groups of people whom I interviewed.

Neither of these texts, as far as I know, has been published anywhere. Of the two, the first is more likely to achieve approval by the academic establishment. The second has a style that is too informal, too personal, and too 'biassed' to fit with the culture of academic literacy. It is also a rewriting of the original which, as Maurice Neville has argued, inevitably means saying something different.[23] For the second is not merely a plain version of the first text; rather, the first is a summary of what 'the report' says, and the second, of what 'the reporter' thinks. These are introductions to two different reports. The second, in terms of writing development, may be seen as more naïve and childlike than the first; for, as Gunther Kress has described, children's early writing has the writer in the foreground; later in their school career they learn that the writing which is rewarded academically is the kind which suppresses the writer from the text. Kress illustrates this move by examples of children's writing using 'the agentless passive' (in the first example above, two of these are linked together in 'it has been found that these causes may be attributed to').[24]

36

Third, even in the more informal writing of personal letters, many students come up against another problem. In theory, they may be freer to write in the style in which they are most at home when they are writing a letter to their sister than when they are writing one to an insurance company. But there is a problem of distance. The sister is well known to the writer; but she is not in the same room. The writer has to guess what mood she will be in when she gets the letter, and what her reaction will be to what is in it. The writer simply does not know whether what she is saying is what her reader wants to read.

All writing, as Frank Smith has pointed out, is a compromise of some kind between the writer and the particular readership they have in mind: 'It is easier for me to scribble but you prefer clear print. I would rather not repeat myself, but you want to hear some things twice.'[25] Another compromise may be between what the writer really wants to write about, and what she imagines her reader might want to read. Sometimes this leads to an internal censor that simply stops the letter being written at all. In certain conditions, this internal censor may be joined by another, external one. Paul Fussell, writing about the 1914–18 war, reports that a soldier writing home had two censors: the officers who routinely censored thousands of letters from the front to relatives at home; and the writer himself. The problem about writing a letter in the midst of appalling suffering and fear was that the writer's central emotions are exactly those which he would least have wanted to inflict on anyone he loved. How could he write about the hideous reality of trench warfare? Or, as Paul Fussell put it: 'What possible good could result from telling the truth?' On the evidence of the letters found in his research, he tells us that the compromise these writers made was to 'fill the page by saying nothing and to offer the maximum number of cliches'.[26]

For a writer to feel any real choice in the style she or he may use, whether in personal or more formal writing, a fourth obstacle has to be overcome. This is the problem of what Frank Smith calls *transcription*: the work of spelling, punctuating and actually producing written script. The difficulty for inexperienced writers, as Frank Smith discusses, is that the preoccupation with *transcription* overcomes their confidence in their *composition*. Their idea of the reader as judge of their technical writing abilities gets in the way of their belief in her or him as colleague, interested in what they have to say as well as how they say it. This was what preoccupied the people doing interviews in Julia Clarke's project (mentioned at the end of chapter 1). It may also have preoccupied numberless soldiers in the First World War, although Paul Fussell does not discuss this possibility. Frank Smith sums up the effects of the preoccupation like this:

> If we expect that someone is likely to assess our ability on the basis of spelling, punctuation, or neatness, then these are aspects of our writing to which we will devote the most attention; and the more we are concerned about the evaluation, the more attention we are likely to commit.[27]

What I have suggested so far, then, is that there are a number of hedges round the freedom of a diffident writer to choose the style she may want. There is, first, the idea that the kind of writing which impresses is long writing, in which the writer's personality is disguised in impersonal phrases. Second, there is the difficulty that writing which is personal, in formal circumstances, is not only regarded as inappropriate; it also exposes the writer to accusations of bias. Third, there is the concern, in more personal writing, that the reader may not want to read what the writer wants to write. And fourth, there is the continuing preoccupation with the look of the writing – how it is spelt, punctuated, laid out and written.

Learning to write confidently means acquiring some choices as to what kind of style and vocabulary the writer would really like to write in: informal or formal, elaborate or plain. Often, teachers imbued with their own sense of the 'proper' way to write for transactional purposes, may suggest that there is a proper (and single) style to write certain kinds of texts. So, for example, one report argues that 'confusing the style needed to write your autobiography with the style needed to apply for a job may not seem important, but for many people it is an expensive mistake'.[28]

It also means acquiring a sense that there really is a reader wanting to read the writing, not as a judge, but as an equal. As I suggest in Part II of this book, community publishing practices have done much to encourage this sense. Writing workshops have brought together writers and readers in a way not made possible in conventional commercial publishing processes. The practice of group members showing each other drafts, giving each other constructive criticism, and reading together reverses, for many people, a whole history of experience in which reading and writing have been isolated and lonely activities. This kind of companionable work is not simple, and, as groups change or get stuck, sometimes difficult. One thing that seems to have resulted, however, is a release from the sense that there is only one proper way of writing about experience, or one style of writing which is superior to another. Alistair Thompson, writing as Development Worker for the national Federation of Worker Writers and Community Publishers, suggests that:

> the artificial distinctions between history, autobiography and fictional writing often blur as people write about their own lives and the life about them in a range of different styles.[29]

The 'blurring' of distinctions between different kinds of writing (history, autobiography and fiction) is partly to do with the writer's purpose, and partly to do with the reader's expectations. A conventional view of history-writing is that is objective; yet social history such as Paul Fussell's depends on personal writings, fiction and poetry. Both writer and reader have to deal with other distinctions, too: those made between 'creative' and 'functional' and between 'formal' and 'informal', discussed in later chapters. Any writing intending to persuade, promote or preach is in the business of stretching the truth for particular purposes. In the same way, writing publicity leaflets and prospectuses for education and training means making choices as to how far to inflate and how much to understate the 'cautious promises' of these opportunities.[30]

The emphasis in this book is on literacy education in groups; and on writing that interweaves with dialogue and conversation between people in those groups. In a helpful collection of studies on language and gender, Valerie Walkerdine writes that the experience of women 'finding a voice' results in 'providing both a place and power to speak'.[31] Such talk results in a making of plural truths (as in my examples of the discussions of colours and about 'pewa' on p. 33), precisely because the mutual support between women in such groups encourages a belief that each of them has something valuable to say.

To sum up: truth in both talk and writing is always conditional. Informal talk and writing is personal and many-sided; and formal talk and writing, as politicians sometimes remind us, can often be 'economical with the truth'. While purposes and audiences dance in front of the writer as she struggles to find the style and the truth of what she wants to say, there is a liberating message for her. Her truth is as valid as anyone else's.

Part II

PRINCIPLES

3

LISTENING TO THE QUESTIONS

In this chapter I want to discuss the principle of *context*. By this I
mean a principle which says: any literacy education works in the
context of people's lives. Literacy itself has both a private and public
context: it is, in our culture, both a personal and social matter. The
things you or I read and write, and the way we read and write them,
are, most of the time, nobody else's business. However, if we want
someone else to agree with us, or to pay us to do a job, sooner or
later we may have to put ourselves on paper: and our uses of literacy
belong to other people, too. Those people make decisions and
judgements on the basis of their assessment of our style, our use of
words and the look of our writing. For example, if I am the national
secretary of a trade union that wants to recruit you as a member, and
the only way you meet me is through the medium of my circular
letter that the branch secretary has sent round to new staff, you will
partly make your decision to join on the basis of how far that letter
persuades you that the union, and I, as its national secretary, would
adequately protect your interests. If I use long-winded sentences,
your view of me may be that I am a windbag. If I (or my secretary)
have misspelt words, and left out capital letters, I am likely to look
like someone who could make mistakes in other ways, too – an
unreliable representative of my members.

A long-winded 'rambling on' about life and incident, if it is
written on the other hand by a long-lost friend, may fulfil exactly
what we have hoped for. The spellings and mistakes of punctuation
in the letter are trivial and unimportant to us. We are simply
overjoyed to get a letter from the friend we have not seen or heard
of for months or years.

Private or public, then, we award different value and status to
different uses of literacy – and hence to the people using it –

43

according to the time, place, and relationship between writer and reader. Adult literacy education, both its promises and its controls, is deeply entangled with these contexts. Its very existence depends on the political context in which it operates. The willingness to allocate any funds at all to this kind of education depends on political judgements. So, in late twentieth-century Britain we find it shadowed by the dominant concerns of a market economy. Publicly funded provision in education and training gives priority to that education and training which demonstrably leads either to jobs or academic qualifications. The 'liberal' tradition of learning for cultural and personal pleasure is now required to justify itself in terms of financial return. Courses in basic education are promoted with the aim of rendering their students more employable, in a context of growing unemployment. Politicians are under pressure to show that this country can successfully compete on a world scale. At local level, this means a pressure, in turn, to show that education and training meets the perceived needs of industry and commerce.

Another political context, often created in opposition to the dominant culture, is that of non-formal education. Historically, despite state reluctance to support them, trade unions, women's groups, and voluntary organisations, in all sorts of contexts, have organised and campaigned for the entitlement to an education on their terms.[1] At the same time, as I argue in later chapters, literacy education which is funded as 'vocational' can be interpreted to mean something more generous than a prescribed set of 'skills to be acquired', if the principles of inquiry, authorship, equality and community are also at work.

The principle of context means that no literacy education is free of either the personal or the political contexts in which it is being offered. To put it positively, the context of people's felt experience in reading and writing is precisely the material from which literacy education grows. The 'context' I discuss in this chapter refers to the moments when literacy, its value and purposes, are the subject of meetings between people both at the point of seeking literacy education and in other social situations.

First, under the heading 'Questions: asked and unasked', I discuss how we invite and listen to questions asked about adult education. Confidently literate people can sometimes experience as much, if not more, embarrassment about the subject of literacy and illiteracy than those for whom reading and writing have always been a struggle. Under 'Literacy: how do we talk about it?' I describe an effort to decide how we can talk about literacy, and with what promises we can advertise and promote its benefits. Third, I link this, to distinctions that need to be made between *needs* and *interests* in discussing the role of adult education; and relate both these to a case study of literacy outreach in the context of a workplace. Finally, I pick out some thoughts on class and education which seem to me particularly relevant to understandings of the context for adult literacy education.

QUESTIONS: ASKED AND UNASKED

At the point of the interview between new student and course tutor, the person asking the questions is most usually the course tutor. The following is a very simplified version of how such an interview may go. The interviewer asks a series of questions (such as: Is there anything that has prompted you to decide to come for help with your reading and writing? Is it mainly reading, or writing that you find hard? Have you been to classes like this before? Is there anything special you know you want to work on? Have you got a job at the moment?), which the interviewee answers. The interviewer then offers some information about the class; and the prospective student may or may not then ask the interviewer some of the questions in her mind.

The answers to our questions help us to give advice and enrol the student in the course most suited to what the prospective student says she is looking for. But the questions she asks us – or wants to ask – are equally important. They help us, on the one hand, to gain a deeper understanding of the context from which this person has decided, at a particular time and place in their lives, to seek out further education for themselves. They also help to give some equilibrium to our meeting. From my own interviewing experience, the questions actually asked by new students concern two things: (i) questions about the context they are about to enter, and (ii) questions about the context they bring with them.

In the first group are questions like: How old are the other students? How many are there? What kind of reading and writing are they dealing with? Is the group all white? There are also a whole lot of other questions, which in my experience are almost never asked at this stage, about the course tutor, such as: What qualifications do you have to teach me? How did you get your education? How old are you? How long have you been doing this job?

In the second group there are questions like: Do you think I will be able to learn in this class? Will I be up to what you will be teaching me? Is the way you will teach going to be like the way anyone else has taught me? How long will it take me to get where I want to? As I've suggested, not many people at the stage of first interview actually voice many of these questions. They may ask, instead, questions about the timing and the fees, and about whether they have to bring anything with them to the class.

This pattern, in my experience, applies to people asking about what might be called more general education – not literacy classes only. Behind both the spoken and the unspoken questions are the personal and social experiences of the person asking them – their story.

The following are just three examples of what I mean, taken from notes of initial inquiries about the programme of community education offered at the Lee Centre in 1983. They are a précis of what, at the time, was a dialogue (between staff and the individuals concerned). For the sake of my argument, I have separated each person's inquiry into their 'question' and the 'story' it comes from:

1 (Question) Do you have to have any qualifications to go on this course?

   (Story) It's not that I've got no education, or anything; but I recently went for a place on a course, and they failed me on my written work. I left school at 14; I've got no complaints really, with my life; it's just that I feel I've got a trapped brain.

2 (Question) How old are the people on your courses? Will I be much older than the others?

   (Story) I know they say it's never too late, but I'm not sure that I'd be clever enough to get into the discussions. I mean, I have my ideas, but I can't put them into words like other people.

3 (Question) Is there anything at your place in the daytime that helps people do a bit of studying?

   (Story) I need something for myself; I don't want to join a parents and toddler session, or anything like that. I need to get away from my kids for a bit. I've not been at school for years, and I feel my brain is going to pot. Mind you, I'm not much good at spelling.

The speakers are asking: How do you get in? Who's there already? When can I find it? Their questions concern course entry requirements, characteristics of other students, and timetable. Their 'stories' express uncertainty as to whether they will fit in or whether they will stick out as less able than everyone else. They also convey the speakers' determination, despite this uncertainty, to find a way to change their present conditions. If the answers they are given are to be persuasive, they must convey a recognition of both the determination and the uncertainty. For literacy education (in the broad sense I am discussing it in this book) to be attractive to speakers like these, much depends on the tone of the answers they get.

Our job, as adult educators, is not only concerned with teaching in a classroom: it is also, always, about how we talk about it. Adult education students, unlike school students, are there because they have made a choice to be. Their decision to make this choice depends on all kinds of other priorities in their lives – and on the way in which we describe the teaching we do. This describing is a whole literacy practice of its own, and entails both print and talk: leaflets, prospectuses and posters on the one hand, and meetings, conversations and interviews, such as those I am discussing, on the other. My argument in this book is that, if we are to be effective in attracting that constituency of people for whom we have designed the courses, what we have to describe is not only what the course is about, but the principles on which we teach it. These descriptions need to be open, and explicitly hospitable to questions. For only by inviting and then listening to questions can we, as providers of an educational opportunity, hope to create appropriate answers.

LITERACY: HOW DO WE TALK ABOUT IT?

One morning in 1975 a woman called Kathryn came into the playgroup in South London where she brought her child every day. She arrived early. The playgroup worker, Kate, was getting out the equipment. Kathryn began telling Kate about her child's illness. She had been to the doctor, who had given her a prescription, which she had collected from the chemist. Kate listened, as she went on pulling toys out of the cupboard. Kathryn held the bottle of tablets, and said 'It's terrible, these doctors' writing. You can't make out what they write.' Kate looked up. 'Here, you have a look at it,' said Kathryn. Kate read the directions on the label. They were handwritten, but not illegible. Kate played a hunch. 'Mm,' she said, 'It's quite a scrawl, isn't it.' She straightened up from setting out the toys and looked at Kathryn. 'I know quite a few people who couldn't read that even if it was written properly,' she went on. 'In fact, a friend of mine says there are quite a lot of people who find reading and writing hard – not stupid people, you understand; just ordinary, intelligent people who just haven't had the chance to feel confident about their reading and writing.' 'Really?' said Kathryn. And Kate went on to mention that this friend ran a literacy scheme not far away. Kathryn showed interest, and Kate went on to say what she knew – about how this literacy scheme treated people as adults, not as children, that people who went along had said they really got a lot out of the classes, and how there were never any tests.

As a result of that conversation, Kathryn made a phone call, went to the literacy scheme, and became a literacy student. A few months later, for the first time in her life, a piece of her writing appeared in print.[2] Later still, she felt sufficiently confident to apply for a training course to qualify her to get employment as a child-care worker.

This is the summary of a real story that a colleague and I used in a series of workshops for community and advice workers in 1986 which we called 'Literacy: how shall we talk about it?' What we were interested to do was to address the *embarrassment of the literate* in talking about literacy and illiteracy. We saw this story as an example of how someone with some information about the attitudes, approaches and teaching principles of an adult literacy scheme could play a practical part in encouraging someone else, whom they had reason to think might find reading and writing a problem, to go and make use of it. We wanted to alert them to the ways in which they could act on their hunches as Kate had done in the scene in the playgroup.[3] We wanted to educate colleagues about our work and how we do it.

We also wanted them to recognise their potential for compounding the stigma of 'illiteracy'. A second story that we used to contrast with first was also based on a real experience. It went like this.

A woman goes into a public library. She is a literacy student, and her tutor has encouraged her to have a go at finding reading material for herself. She has not used a library before. She goes up to the library counter. There are a couple of people waiting behind her. 'Could you tell me,' she says quietly, 'where I could find any easy books for adults to read?' The librarian looks up from indexing some cards, and says in a clear voice, without hesitation: 'Easy books for adults? You'll find them listed in our catalogue: it's just over there.'

In discussions with the community workers, health visitors and librarians who attended these workshops, we invited them to notice all the features of this scene: the other people at the counter, hearing the librarian's answer; the difficulty the woman had with confident reading and the implication which, with attention, was clearly behind her question – that she would not be likely to find reading catalogues easy. The workshops were a kind of 'consciousness raising' strategy (and were followed, among other things, by follow -up in-service training for library staff, which they requested). The librarian in this scene, had she herself been part of the group and paused to reflect on her own words, would very probably have felt mortified. The point of the exercise was not to single out as villain a wicked individual who had failed to see the humiliation she had caused in the person on the other side of the counter. Rather, our purpose was to use the story – which is, without any doubt, repeated countless times up and down the country in other contexts – as an example of two things. On the one hand, there is the pre-vailing and damning view that those who can't read are thick. On the other is the result of such a view: that anyone who is revealed publicly as having difficulty in reading is open to ridicule. The student who reported the story reported that she had, indeed, wished the floor would open and swallow her up. She, far more than the librarian could be, was acutely aware of the other people in the queue behind her and the whole environment of books and reading.

What could the librarian have said? How could she have said it differently? Was there, in fact, any way for that scene to be replayed without some acute embarrassment being felt by someone? How many of the people in the queue actually paid enough attention to the exchange to register the meaning of the woman student's question? What did they feel? For the woman in question, the conviction was that they must immediately feel contempt for her. Perhaps one or two of them felt embarrassment. Precisely because they were aware that she might believe that of them, and because they wanted to avoid the slightest impression that contempt was what they did feel, they might have turned away, and pretended they hadn't heard. (It is important to affirm at this point that librarians as a profession have played a key role in promoting adult education in this country: playing host to student groups visiting both in and out of public opening hours, and demystifying the bookish rooms; promoting opportunities through their information and advice services; and liaising with adult education locally to ensure that their information is accurate.)

Both playgroups and libraries are contexts in which literacy is actively used and talked about. Beyond these buildings and settings are the social maps in which they are located: in the case of both these stories, an inner-city one. The same buildings and settings, in a remote country village, have different social surroundings; and in making outreach efforts or advice links for literacy, we have to be careful that our zeal to evangelise does not blind us to these differences. Outreach efforts for literacy in this country have taken many forms, over the years and in all sorts of different contexts. Pablo Foster, in an article describing publicity efforts in the Scottish Highlands[4], primarily to recruit volunteer tutors, reminds us of the physical distances and close communities characteristic of rural contexts. He suggests that it is a combination of this paradox – distance and closeness – which may act to deter people from revealing their difficulties with reading and writing. He also refers to the 'passionately independent lives' of people in this huge rural area. At the time of writing, he reports that of a population of 190,000 in the area, just 123 people were registered as literacy students – and 135 as literacy volunteers. He commented:

> Comparatively few people in need find the courage to break cover, and whereas Glasgow has a shortage of tutors, the Highlands tend to have a shortage of students. In some areas it seemed easier to stalk a deer than a student.

His conclusion, at the time, suggested strategies such as ours: 'Educating the public at large, to reduce stigma, is still a necessary task.'

NEEDS AND INTERESTS

The idea of there being 'people in need' has been a feature of social policy for some time. Adult education has often been seen as setting out to 'meet the needs' of given groups or individuals. In an essay entitled 'The myth of meeting needs in adult education and community development'[5] Paul Armstrong offers what I find to be a useful account of the policy context in which literacy workers (such as myself or Pablo Foster) have been situated. Ideas about 'deprivation' and 'disadvantage' mushroomed in the late 1960s and early 1970s, with the publication of the Seebohm report[6] giving rise to the national Community Development Project's strategy of combating urban decay with community action. Armstrong

summarises a subsequent change in thinking – from an idea about
'need' to one which focused on 'interests'. He does this by first
suggesting a sequence of three sets of causes to which poverty and
urban deprivation had been attributed: (i) the poor themselves; (ii)
poor communications within the local authority bureaucracy; and
(iii) fundamental social and economic inequalities within
contemporary capitalism.

Policy in adult education has not moved in a chronological line
from the first of these positions to the third. However, the thinking
which has underlain adult literacy education since 1970 has moved
between all three. Armstrong argues that those seeing deprivation as
caused by the deprived looked to remedial measures to remove or
compensate for deprivation. Those, on the other hand, who
regarded poor communications as the problem proposed organised
community action as a solution. Those, finally, who were primarily
concerned with inequality argued for measures in the interests of
the working class.

The idea of meeting needs, he suggests, is based on an
assumption that those attempting to meet them know what they are.
The question then becomes: are we attempting to meet a whole lot
of different individual needs, calling for individual answers, or are
we trying to meet the needs of a group? And further: are the needs
those coming from within or are they needs defined and/or imposed
by forces outside a person?

One person's 'need' for literacy, in a practical sense, may be a
'need' to write a note to someone or a 'need' to read an instruction
book for a new washing machine. For a particular person in a
particular situation, these needs may feel urgent. The 'need' for this
person to acquire the literacy skills to do these things themselves,
however, may not be great at all.

The context within which someone decides for themselves that
they have an increased need for, or interest in, their own literacy
development is often one of recent change or loss. Interesting
research by David Barton and Sarah Padmore, who interviewed
twenty people in Lancaster about their uses of literacy, suggested
that many people have well-established networks of help with
reading and writing (often reciprocated by some other help they
give in exchange). Two of those they spoke to, despite feeling that
their own literacy was not as competent as they would have liked,
were sources of literacy support to others. (One woman helped
neighbours with both advice on their marriage problems and the

forms that 'would follow on the problem'. Another, who was known for her neat handwriting, was quite often called upon to do artwork for signs and posters in the local community. 'Neither of these women', the writers report, 'felt totally confident about their own literacy skills').

It is precisely because such networks exist, this research suggests, that difficulties with literacy do not feel like a 'need' for literacy education. It is only when such supports are removed that the decision to find other support (in the form of a literacy class) is made.

> It is important to emphasise that often, because these networks exist, problems do not arise. People live within these networks and go about their lives without particularly identifying problems with reading and writing. *Often, it was when these networks were disrupted that people were confronted with problems and this was sometimes given as a reason for coming to basic education classes* [my italics].[7]

The 'contexts' for literacy interests reported by policies for adult basic education are proposed, by definition, by literate educators. It is encouraging, then, to reread a policy document published in 1979, which says:

> Adult basic education is generally described as consisting of certain specific skills. That is the educator's view of it. For the participant, readiness to come forward will come from some context within his [*sic*] own life.[8]

The examples of the contexts then suggested are, however, limited to a catalogue of literacy requirements for work, family life, travel and leisure, and a general heading of 'citizenship'. The individuals and groups for whom basic education is proposed in this report are characterised as deprived. It should come as no surprise, then (following Armstrong's analysis) that they are also seen as having not interests but needs. ('These communities have *special group needs* . . . awareness of *these needs* has prompted . . . some people of West Indian background *have different needs* . . . .'.) The clearest example of the 'need' view of prospective participants is in the section on 'the unemployed':

> Although the unemployed are not *in need* of basic education as a category, the literacy campaign and the courses

sponsored by the Training Services Division have shown that there is again a proportionately *high incidence of need* for basic education amongst the unemployed . . . The Holland Report 'Young People and Work' . . . has pointed to *the need to* extend the opportunities for daytime study for unemployed adolescents.

The people supplying the evidence of 'need' are those who appeared as a result of the campaign and the courses: people who became students, and who also became categorised as having, not networks of support, or the capacity to supply that support, but 'needs'. By 1979 the ground had moved from the needs of 'adult illiterates' to those of students. As I have already argued in Part I, 'there is no guarantee' (in Mary Hamilton's words) 'that those who come forward for tuition are representative of those who do not'.[9] Now that we have more mature research studies, both of students' uses of literacy outside the classroom and of people's literacy uses, whether or not they are enrolled as students, we can confidently shed all talk of 'needs'. The ground we stand on now is that of *interests*.

CONTEXT AND OUTREACH

'Outreach', a word originating in community education policy-writing of the 1970s, essentially means three things at once: research, consultation and action. The outreach worker goes out with questions, and an intention to provide some kind of appropriate answer to them. The guiding principle for both questions and answer is that of consultation. Those she meets with and of whom she asks her research questions are also those who will influence, shape and have some control over the action she takes. For example: the outreach worker meeting with women living in a particular estate goes to where they meet, asks direct or indirect questions about what facilities they would like to improve or change their situation, and then brings to them the resources which will make some of that improvement or change possible. These resources may be a tutor or group-worker, some equipment, some transport (possibly the use of a minibus) and, sometimes, premises.

The questions and answers, however, often flow both ways. As I suggested at the beginning of this chapter, education outreach raises a variety of questions from the people who the educator is meeting. While this is true, as I've suggested, for any outreach in any context, it is, in my experience, particularly true for the literacy educator doing development work in the context of workplaces. Talking about the uses of literacy and asking about people's interests in developing their own is, as I have also suggested, a touchy subject. Kate's conversation with Kathryn (pp. 47–8) was possible, in the context of their familiar meeting place (the playgroup) largely because Kate knew of an adult literacy scheme and had learned about literacy work. (At the time, my children attended her playgroup and Kate and I had had several conversations about the work I did.) Had Kate not known of a possible 'solution' to the hidden questions behind Kathryn's query about the writing on the label, she would not have had, I suggest, the confidence to extend the conversation to the general subject of reading and writing, and then to the particular information about a local centre where, she knew, adults with difficulties in literacy took action to resolve them. Her description of the kind of people that she knew from me attended literacy classes anticipated questions Kathryn might have had about how she herself might be seen in that context: such questions as the three I quoted earlier (p. 46), about whether she would fit in or stick out.

Outreach, 'cold', to a group of people who have not declared any need for literacy or any interest in improving their own, follows a similar pattern. The outreacher goes to where those people already are. She observes and asks questions about the kind of literacy they have to handle on a routine basis. She then describes something general about the kind of approach to literacy teaching she herself uses, and her experience of the people who become literacy students. The way is then open for the group she is meeting to ask their own questions. The important thing is that the questions they ask derive from their own context, experience and knowledge. The questions she may ask them are asked to help her clarify the ways in which a course she is there to propose could best fit that context.

This pattern, in my view, is also that which works best for individual interviews. In practice, I suspect a large number of further and adult education course tutors do interview prospective students in this way, rather than the simple method I described earlier. This is not, however, the conventional expectation of such interviews, particularly when there are a limited number of places on a course and selection is necessary. (Nor is it the convention in research methodology recommended for sociological interviews: in these the researcher is expected to ask all the questions, and resist any attempts by the interviewee to ask her about her experience or opinions.)[10]

In 1986 I spent twelve weeks researching and consulting with another group of employees and their managers, with a view to providing and teaching a course in work time to be called 'Fresh start'. The employer was a local authority (Lewisham Borough Council Architects' Department). The employees were cleaning staff. The project was initiated by the Council's women's training officer, Rosemary Towler. As a result of her work and mine, two courses were held in 1987, with twelve women on each course. Each lasted ten weeks, with two two-hour sessions per week, from 6.45–8.45 a.m. There are some examples of the work done on the two courses in subsequent chapters. Here, I want to focus on the questions I was asked at the development stage, and what these have to do with the principle of context.

Initially, I met with the training officer to discuss plans. She wanted, she said, to provide training opportunities for women manual workers in the Council. The Council had an equal opportunities policy: manual-worker training was already under way; her role was to ensure that women manual workers – many part-time and shift-working – were also assured genuine opportunities for training. She had attended one of our workshops, 'Literacy: how can we talk about it?', and was particularly anxious to enable women who could not read and write confidently to have a full share of these opportunities. She proposed working with a particular sector of staff for whom there had been no training opportunity until then: cleaners. There were, at that time, some 180 cleaning staff employed by the Architects' Department. Rosemary had recently run a short training course for cleaning supervisors in supervision skills, which had gone well. As things turned out, this proved to be a major factor in the success of the 'Fresh start' courses for cleaners themselves: the supervisors were eager to promote the pleasures of training to their staff, having had a recent and positive experience of it themselves.

We had two meetings (in August and September 1987) with the nine supervisors and the Department's superintendent. Guided by comments in the first, I brought to the second the draft of a leaflet inviting interest in a course, and several possible course titles. Of the six I brought in, the one which the meeting favoured was that used for one of the GLC courses in 1985, 'Fresh start for women manual workers'. (The problem of course title is never a simple one. I still treasure the one I used for the first such course I ran: 'A new course in work time.'[11] More recently, the title 'Paperwork made easy' was chosen for a course for another group of manual workers.) The supervisors offered to be distribution points for the leaflet, when it was printed. We agreed the idea of an information meeting open to all cleaners to attend, whether they were interested in the course or not. The leaflet was primarily, then, an invitation to this.

Between that September meeting with the supervisors and the November open meeting, I then had eight other meetings in the buildings where cleaners worked, with supervisors convening small groups of cleaners to meet me in each case. I brought batches of the leaflet with me to give to those I met, and asked them to pass them on to others.

It's important at this point to quote from the text of the leaflet itself, in order to recognise the significance of the questions I was asked. The front said:

> You are invited to a meeting on Friday November 7th, at 8.0 a.m. at Lewis Grove Training Centre, to hear about FRESH START – a new course for women cleaning staff.

Inside were these words:

WHAT IS 'FRESH START'?
It is a new course run by the Council for women cleaning staff.
WHEN WILL IT BE?
On Wednesday and Friday mornings, from 7.0 to 9.0 am for ten weeks, starting in January 1987.
WHAT WILL THE COURSE OFFER?
– practice in writing and speaking up
– information on how the Council works
– time to talk about what you know
– ideas for study or training that you may want to go on to
WHO CAN APPLY FOR A PLACE ON 'FRESH START'?
You – if you are a woman and work as a cleaner for the Council's architects' department. There will be 12 places on the course. Your job is safe, and there will be no loss of pay while you are on the course.

If you think you are
– too old

– no good at spelling or reading
– too busy,
THINK AGAIN!
* Women of any age are welcome
* the course will help you brush up your English
* this is your time, for you – and you have earned it!

Want to know more?
Please come to the meeting on Friday 7th November – and find out what it is all about from Rosemary Towler (Women's Training Officer) and Jane Mace and Tara McArthur (course tutors) – or, if you can't make that, please give your name to your supervisor. She will pass it on to Jane and Tara.

There is NO TEST to join the course; but Jane will get in touch with every woman who says she would like to apply – to have a personal chat.

Readers experienced in drafting publicity for courses will notice that there is little here about the actual content of the course proposed. You may also notice that the leaflet by definition presumes an ability to read in the recipient. This is why the support and enthusiasm of the supervisors, as distributors of it, was important to the success of the exercise. If need be, they could tell a woman what the leaflet said, without her having to read it. They could also make the difference between the idea being attractive, and it seeming like yet another bit of bureaucracy sent from the office people. As one supervisor put it, in the August meeting:

I mean, if I say, 'Oh shit, look at this rubbish they've sent us now', they won't be interested, will they? Whereas if I say, 'Here, take a look at this, this looks interesting', they might feel different.

It was partly in order to make its message known to all staff concerned, including those for whom English literacy might be limited, that I had arranged to visit the buildings in which the women worked and talk to them about it. In other words, I set out on the outreach exercise with the expectation of being asked some questions. But I also wanted to learn for myself something of the context from which any course participants would be coming.

All the eight meetings that autumn took place in the women's working hours (between 7 and 9 a.m.), in the buildings they normally worked in. Most of the meetings lasted twenty minutes. Women left their hoovers and buckets, and sat down or leaned against the door, smoking, talking to each other, some listening to me, some not. I was usually introduced by the supervisor, if she was there. All supervisors had to cover several buildings, however, so sometimes I went in and had to introduce myself from scratch. There were between eight and a dozen women at each meeting. Essentially the questions I was asked in all these discussions were three: Who will do my work if I come on the course? What is the purpose of the course? What good will it do me if I come on the course?

It's a useful exercise to apply these questions to any course offer in adult and further education (using the word 'work' in the first question in the broad sense, as well as 'paid work'). It's useful, too, to work out an appropriate strategy for dealing with the question: 'What good will it do us?' which one woman followed by saying: 'We already have our hobbies. I know I have. And they won't give us another job. I've tried.' I say 'strategy for dealing with', because actually attempting simply to answer the question in one go may not be the best strategy. The course in question was offering no certificate and no guarantee. A solution consistent with issues of representation I discussed in Part I is that which employs quotation from members of similar courses elsewhere. I found this kind of answer appeared to be useful:

> Well, people who have been on courses like this have said things like: 'You gain a lot of confidence in yourself.' I know several people who find they learn a lot by having the time to sit down and discuss things, and get a bit more practice in writing – letters, especially.

Above all, it was important in these discussions to say, even if I was never asked to say, that the course positively welcomed anyone who could not read and write easily. There is in my experience no simple way of saying this; it is something that we must keep trying to put into words if we mean anything by workplace literacy.

CLASS AND LITERACY: SOME THEMES

'Workplace literacy' is a catchphrase which means different things to different people. By choosing to focus many of the examples in this context, I do not mean to imply that literacy education for people not in employment is no longer important. Rather, I suggest that the context of a workplace actually illustrates in a concentrated form some of the attitudes to class and education which are prevalent in general in our society. It is significant to note that Workbase, the project which pioneered workplace literacy education, first began in the very place where higher education and learning intersected with low status work and poor training opportunities. Its origins lie in the anger felt by a trade union official working with manual staff in the University of London on finding that one of his shop stewards 'couldn't read or write and was working in this academic institution. I said it was a scandal.'[11] The 'scandal' is the close proximity of extremes: the illiterate employed by an organisation representing the summit of literacy; the implied denial of an employee's most basic rights to education, in the very place purporting to offer rights to a higher kind of learning for other people.

The cleaners and I sometimes met in large open-plan offices, filled with the evidence of the bureaucratic literacy which for some of them was a foreign language. But not all. Women who work part-time at night or in the early morning as cleaners are by no means all 'illiterate' in the sense of being without the confidence to read. Many who had considerable competence in their writing and some qualifications, applied for a place on the 'Fresh start' course. The message which the outreach work and publicity attempted to convey was that the course content offered staff development, rather than 'basic skills'. It was, at the same time, a deliberate attempt to make available to one sector of staff a training opportunity in the knowledge that both non-readers and fluent readers could openly work together on 'writing and speaking up'. In the next chapter I shall be discussing how this approach implies a syllabus which is sketched in outline before the course, and only fully written when the course is over – for it implies that the participants themselves make the curriculum

Manual workers, as working class people, are only too aware of class attitudes towards their position in the work hierarchy. Their work is low-status and commonly assumed to require a low level of skill. This leads to assumptions about a correspondingly low level of intelligence. Anyone coming into this context with an offer of specific education or training for this group of workers, therefore, is in extreme danger of appearing patronising and arrogant; and to some people, in that project, that is exactly how I may have appeared. The co-operation, interest and control of workers' elected representatives – their trade union officers – is always important in any enterprise aspiring to create trust and express respect for the context and existing knowledge of the people concerned.[12] (In the case I have been discussing, the NUPE shop steward was consulted at the planning stages of the courses, expressed support for the idea, and accepted an invitation from the first course group to meet them at the end of the course.) As the 'scandal' continues, and an unequally large share of resources are consistently given to the education and training of the higher paid staff, the work of promoting such courses can only be done adequately if these inequalities are recognised as integral to their context.

Literacy, with its association with intelligence, is a highly sensitive subject. Courses offering literacy to manual workers, then, however well intentioned, enter a highly charged context – in which jobs are being cut, pay is low, and the demand for increased productivity is being added to an already overstretched workforce. With no tradition of any training ever being offered, and an invitation to participate in a course which talks of reading and writing, and communication – let alone uses the word 'literacy' itself – people employed in low-status work have every reason to feel like this group:

> We were suspicious of the leaflets inviting us to take a day off a week for ten weeks. It was strange to be asked to study subjects which interested us and could be of our own choosing. What was it all about? What was the Gaffer's angle – giving us time off with no obvious advantage to him? We who swept the city streets, cleaned toilets, did the filing, mowed grass verges, and the numerous humdrum, irksome, important, but under-valued jobs which have to be done by that ill-fated 'somebody'. No-one ever gave us 'owt.[13]

There were, as I've said, a hundred and eighty women working as cleaners at the time I worked on the project in Lewisham. Of these, we (I and my co-tutor) met with some sixty in the preliminary meetings and the open meeting. Thirty-five asked for places on the 'Fresh start' course. Fifteen came to the first course; a core of twelve attended all ten weeks; and a further twelve attended the second. The uses these and other manual staff I have taught on subsequent courses made of literacy were varied; or, in the jargon, the courses were 'mixed ability'. All could read and write something; few read or wrote habitually for more than the essentials.

The exercise, I emphasise, was not one of detecting a 'basic skills need' in this sector of employees, but of providing a staff development opportunity for them to shape, in the knowledge that literacy – ease with reading and writing – was an open and explicit item on the course agenda. Many who were known to have trouble with reading and writing did not show interest in the course being offered. Of the people who did not meet me, and those who did but then did not ask for a place on the course, and the small number of those who came to the course but did not stay, an unknown number may have been in the position of wanting some kind of course to help their literacy but not finding this one attractive. If the project had been attempting to 'meet the needs' of these people, then this could indeed be seen as a failure. My purpose was, as best I could, to elicit and work with the interests of the people concerned; using the questions they asked me, as well as those I asked them, to guide me.

The contexts reported in the film *Liberating literacy*, described in chapter 1, included a prison, a women's centre, a job club, an open-learning centre, a community bookshop and an independent basic education college. The inequality of class and literacy is felt differently by different people in these different contexts. Many arrive in literacy education with feelings not of anger but of fear, conscious always of the possibility that their difficulties will be discovered and they will not get a job, will lose a job, or dare not aspire to a better job.

Anger and fear sometimes go together. This account by an auxiliary nurse is an example:

> I get this inadequate feeling. To be unable to write classifies
> you as an idiot. People make fun of it; it's a joke. It restricts you
> in the way you earn your living. I've never dared upgrade
> myself in case I make a fool of myself.

She felt 'inadequate'; but she also saw other people as doing the negative 'classifying'. It is a combination of frustration with herself and frustration with other people's prejudices; a combination which is probably the single most important barrier to any individual's decision to take part in literacy education. For such a decision means finding the energy to make a challenge to attitudes which are inside the learner's head as well as in other people's.

In the same report from which this quotation comes[14] is a case study of another woman, who did make such a decision, named as Brenda, introduced as follows:

> She had been working part-time as a cleaner at a local adult education centre. When her children went to school she decided to work full-time and was offered the opportunity to take on the job of cleaner-in-charge at the centre. The job involved writing cleaning schedules for all the part-timers and reports of all the work undertaken. Brenda was very apprehensive about these new tasks, but willing to enrol for an evening class.

Brenda and the tutor worked out a plan for her literacy work, focusing on the writing and spelling she wanted to handle more confidently. Brenda came three times a week to a class where group activities were going on, but chose to work on her own at first. Later, 'as her confidence grew, she began to take much more notice of what was going on in the group and at an appropriate time was encouraged to join in'. The author (who is unnamed) tells us that Brenda 'gradually got drawn into several group activities', and got 'very involved one evening when the group was writing a letter of complaint about the lighting in the car park'.

After three months, coming three times a week, Brenda had made noticeable progress and felt able to do what she had set out to do: the literacy at work of schedule and work reports. What is striking about the end of the story is the glimpse, not only of Brenda's progress in the usual sense, but also a new defiance. Brenda had had an interest in developing her literacy. She had come along and done it. In the process, she had also developed a change in attitude: the fact that her writing was not perfect *no longer mattered to her.*

> At the end of the third month Brenda left the class declaring herself well satisfied with her progress. The tutor pointed out a spelling error on the final report *but Brenda said the occasional one didn't matter.*

This section has been a necessarily brief sketch of some of the class issues which concern the context of adult literacy education. Changes like Brenda's – from apprehension to assertion – are personal changes; but they are more than a change in an individual's confidence. Her writing at work is other people's business, as well as her own; so, too, is her attitude towards it. Her change in attitude is a political change, for it will certainly pose a challenge to other people's attitudes, too.

4

THE TEACHER-RESEARCHER

In Part I of this book I questioned the assumption that literacy, to those for whom it has not been easy, should be something to which all would aspire. In the previous chapter I discussed the principle of *context* in promoting literacy's attractions. Attention to the personal and social contexts in which anyone uses literacy, and to the context in which any education work may be offered, is essential, I have argued, to any meaningful outreach work. In this chapter, I suggest how this attention to context also extends to that of the classroom. The principle of *inquiry* in the initial stages of a course, adopted by the teacher, encourages in turn the idea of students as researchers, too. By this principle students are not merely consumers, but creators of the course curriculum, and the teacher is a learner in this process.

In the first section of this chapter 'Researching the interest' I suggest that the research stance of outreach work can inform the planning stages of both class and course. In the next section, 'Context and menus', I suggest how a group may contribute their own ingredients to the usual menu of literacy education for adults. The third section, 'Researching the answers' contrasts the teacher-instructor approach to that of teacher-researcher. Finally, 'Words and contradictions' gives examples of ways in which students can be encouraged to explore sometimes conflicting attitudes to their learning, and to collaborate in researching, in talk, some of the vocabulary they want to use in writing.

RESEARCHING THE INTEREST

Teaching approaches, in different contexts and disciplines, vary widely across a continuum. At one end is the teacher who walks into a classroom with, as it were, a blank sheet of paper. She sees her job to be to start from where the students are. This position can either mean she works from every individual's separate interests and expressed needs, or from themes and ideas elicited from the group as a whole. In adult literacy education this can mean, as it did for Brenda (in the previous chapter), the individual being guided to discover and make their own text for study. If the person finds reading any text a major problem, the method often used is that known as 'language experience', by which the tutor acts as scribe, and with the student's agreement, writes a series of sentences drawn from something they have said. This is then the student's reading matter, and basis for writing development.

In the case of a group, a similar approach is used (to borrow Paulo Freire's term) to 'generate a theme' of common interest, for which reading and writing activities are collected and developed (examples occur later in this chapter and in chapter 5). The 'blank sheet' approach is also, in part, the approach offered in open-learning centres or language workshops, although, since it depends on there being already a set of resources and materials, this may seem contradictory. These, however, are not prepared precisely for a particular group session, but are there for individual students to use, with guidance, depending on the immediate interests they express. The tutor waits for these to be expressed before suggesting the choice they might then make from these materials.

At the other end of the continuum is the teacher who, before entering the classroom, has put a lot of work into writing a syllabus, worksheets, notes for a presentation and/or talk that she will give. There is a series of items or subjects to be 'got through' within a given timetable. Students produce writing which she reads and returns, with comments, marks or assessment notes. This approach, at its extreme, is an imitation of the academic lecture, supported by reading-list and marked essay. In contrast to the teacher with the blank sheet, this teacher has a 'prepared script'. A version of this approach is found in those courses designed to identify, improve and assess specific skills, with standardised tests determining the curriculum to be followed.

This description is, of course, a very simplified version of reality. As Deryn Holland found in her research on methods of assessment in literacy education,[1]

Teaching to a 'test' is considered inappropriate in student

centred approaches to basic education, in which each student is to be treated as an individual learner and individual needs met in appropriate ways.

This opposition to testing and what I am calling 'the prepared script', however, appears to be based on an entirely individual version of learning, an impression confirmed by what Deryn Holland says next: 'To generalise the learning experience by constraining students to a common curriculum is, according to this position, to construct a paradox.'

Paradoxes are indeed at the heart of adult literacy education. Individual 'needs' and collective interests struggle for time. This is probably why both of the teachers I have described, in reality, borrow from the methods of the other. The teacher with the 'prepared script' will adapt it to the particular students she is working with. The teacher with the 'blank sheet of paper' will from time to time offer a didactic speech on the best way to do something, and frequently offer responses to individual students' learning needs. Brenda's tutor was, apparently, both working with her individual programme of work and enabling a group to do group work (very possibly prepared in advance by the tutor) – which, at one stage, Brenda chose to join (see pp. 62–3). Most literacy educators move between blank sheets and prepared scripts, and if asked to say where we belonged, would put ourselves somewhere on the continuum between them.

Some of what has been called the 'post-basic literacy' work in the last decade or so has evolved a model of work which combines both syllabus and unplanned methods. This has developed along with the strategy of the single intake course: the self-contained part-time course, over a period of weeks, planned on the basis of a group of students who all start at the same time, keep coming regularly and stop coming at a point decided in advance as being the end. This model, of course, has a longer history in further education courses (such as the Pre-Tops then Preparatory courses)[2] than in adult basic education provided in the voluntary sector or in adult institutes.

Adult basic educators like me were, in the 1970s, used to teaching weekly classes, planning 'on the hoof' for one week at a time, in circumstances where the composition of the group was constantly changing. The large majority of adult literacy work still takes this form. Here, as an example, is an outline of two weeks of a class we could call the 'Thursday evening "Brush up your English" class':

Week 1. There are six students in the group. Of these, two started last month, three have been attending for over a year, one is coming tonight for the first time, another recently rejoined the group after an absence of six months.

Week 2. This time there are nine students, of whom only four are the same as the previous week. Of the first two, one has got an evening job and can't come any more. One of the longer-stayers has flu and does not turn up. The newcomer does not reappear for her second attendance. The student who has rejoined brings a friend. A newcomer arrives half-way through the session. Two students have been transferred to this class as theirs has just been closed down.

Student-centred planning in these conditions means a lot of attention to individuals. Each person has different histories and purposes for the learning they want to do; each also has a different experience of being a member of this particular group. A group activity in which everyone has a part can often boil down to twenty minutes in the middle when the group can be asked to focus on the same piece of reading or discussion. Much of my *Learning from experience* (1980) was addressed to ideas that groups in this situation could do together, as a means to share some of their interests and get comfortable with each other.

By contrast, the 'return to study' course and the communication skills course in the workplace have a beginning and an end, and intend to collect at the start a whole group who will remain with the course for its entirety. The duration of such courses will vary from 30 to 150 hours (usually 4–6 hours a week). For the course tutors or trainers wanting to maintain students' contribution to the curriculum, the work of planning is no longer preparing work from one week to the next, adapting the plan on the spot to changes in the group. Instead, they face the dilemma of how to prepare, plan and promote a whole course as attractive and relevant, on the one hand, while on the other hand being willing to follow the lead of the people who then take part in it and to change the plan in the middle.

In chapter 3, I discussed the issue of talking about literacy at a stage when there is a hunch that someone may have an interest in finding a course which would help them develop their own, and the 'cautious promises' we make in outreach and written publicity. Here, I want to describe something of the talk and writing involved in making the course curriculum itself, after the process of interviewing and offering places to students has been done.

In 1980, at the Lee Centre, we started our first 'return to study' course. Inspired by one with the same title which had already been running at the Friends Centre, Brighton, we called it 'New Horizons'. The course timetable was two sessions a week for three terms. Conscious, from our experience of adult literacy work, that many people worked alternating shifts and were not able to attend at the same time every week, we planned the same course to run concurrently in the morning and in the evening – with the idea that students, if they needed to, could alternate from week to week and still keep up with the same course. After two years of running it this way, we abandoned this scheme, in favour of a one-day-a-week course for two terms. We also, after considerable discussion, redesigned it as a women-only course.

Before the first 'New Horizons' course, the course team of four tutors planned, in advance, a syllabus for the whole three terms of the course. This was intensely complicated, but in many ways, once the courses began, unusually comforting – after the irregularity and unpredictability of the weekly literacy teacher's experience, the idea of knowing what we would be teaching three weeks (let alone three terms) in advance seemed astonishingly liberating. Life on the course, however, led us to adapt the plans we had: some topics needed more time, others less; and students proposed extra subjects we had not included.

So before the second course began, in 1981, we planned it a term at a time. In 1982, when the course had changed to be daytime and women-only, I recall that we were more modest still: we planned the first five weeks, then put ideas to the students and asked for their preferences as to the rest of the course. Subsequent courses I have taught, on different timetables, have had echoes of the same process: intense and detailed planning for the first go at the course, diminishing, as teaching confidence increased, to planning for only the first part of the course, allowing scope for reshaping of the rest by the group itself. I say 'teaching confidence', because it takes considerable confidence and experience to prepare for this kind of unpredictable work. The important thing is to maintain, for course members, a clarity as to the purpose of what they do next.

Then comes the first meeting of the course participants. At this stage, many course tutors plan some open discussion about previous experiences of education and of work, paid or unpaid. The purpose for this discussion is, first and foremost, to allow the group to let each other know something of themselves. It is also to educate and inform the teacher about their existing knowledge and attitudes to the course they have now joined. It is always important, however, that the discussion's boundaries are clear. Participants are being invited, not forced, to tell something of their experience. This sense of invitation can be expressed by reading from other writings which may describe familiar attitudes or feelings. For some time, in my teaching, I used extracts from autobiographies from community publications which described experiences of schooling and employment. The positive effects of using other writings as well as those of the group itself are both the sense of recognition these can offer to the students' own experience, and a freedom from the pressure on them to reveal more of it than they might want to.

Later, I found it felt important to relate these accounts to others: those expressed in policy papers or by educationalists, or in fiction. It seemed increasingly important to make the relationship between the personal and the social and historical context.

CONTEXT AND MENUS

The first workplace course I taught was in 1984; the second, in 1987. Looking back, I can see this change in emphasis from the personal to the social. In the first course, the early reading was an autobiographical piece on leaving school: in the second, it was a selection of views about education and training, combining fiction with policy writing. However, along with this shift was one which moved towards more activity in which the group would make its own reading material. In the second course, we did an exercise (described in more detail in the final section of this chapter) called 'I want to learn/I am good at', the results of which were photocopied and brought back for reading the following week. In the second course, too, I asked in the first week if the group would be interested to make their own magazine – a practice common to the adult literacy group meeting weekly over several months, but not something easily to be achieved in a course only ten weeks in length. The students all said yes. One of the effects of this decision was that two members of this group who had done almost no writing by week eight of the course were encouraged to do so, not by me, but by others in the group – pointing out they would otherwise not have anything in the magazine.

As it happens, both courses were funded in part from departmental and college research funds for which I had applied, as well as the employer's training budget; in some sense my role was meant to be that of researcher (which is possibly why I kept such copious notes on the courses). Both had single intakes of twelve students, lasted for ten weeks, and were team-taught. I single them out for comparison to illustrate some shifts in emphasis in my own work towards a more confident 'teacher-researcher' position. In my planning for the first course, I was preoccupied with ensuring that, from the students' point of view, it would feel practical. I was anxious not to waste their time. I was partly guided by some of the things they had told me, in pre-course interviews, that they found hard to do in their reading and writing. At the same time, I was concerned to demonstrate that members of a group such as this one were not seen by the employer as lacking in skills to deal with the organisation's communication systems, but rather that they were capable of contributing ideas for how these systems could be improved.

The first three weeks of the 1984 course included: a reading called 'When I leave school' by Pat Dallimore,[3] to release discussion about experiences of schooling and ideas about work; and study of diagrams of the plan of the building, pictures of the posters and signs in the corridors and rooms.

We also spent a session examining information leaflets about the local council, and facts and figures about local employment. This was included partly because the course offered something about 'help with maths' and the topic seemed to be a useful one for critical discussion. (I recall an atmosphere of polite boredom with this session.) Also introduced mainly as a 'functional' idea, we had a session in which we pored over maps of the area, of the country and of the world, as a means to help people check their understanding of geography and practice further basic numeracy in calculating distances and so on. (It was this session, of the two, which was the more lively, and led to some interest in writing about personal geographies and childhoods in southern Italy, Ireland and the Caribbean.) Writing activity in the first two weeks of this course included short pieces about first experiences of work.

The first two weeks' work in the 'Fresh start' courses which I co-ordinated and taught three years later for Lewisham Council were broadly similar, but had some differences:

Week 1. (a) Introducing our partner; ideas about education and training; I want to learn/I am good at.

(b) Maps, measurement; writing, 'Sundays'; agreement to make a course magazine.

Week 2. (a) Discussion about children, and about spelling; writing, about pictures.

(b) Reading back writings; 'slow' and 'fast' word-game and writing.

In comparing notes of these two courses, the change in approach between the first and the second seems mostly to have been a change in my teaching confidence. I was more confident to wait until the group of people were in the classroom with me, to know whether they would actually want to have a way of dealing with statistics, or understanding the structure of the Council. The exercise to write about Sundays, the work with pictures, the reading back of writing, and the 'slow' and 'fast' word-game in this course were all activities with a collaborative approach. They all (as I shall later discuss in more detail) expected students to work together and make the work themselves. The proposal to make a magazine became a project which created many of the purposes for later course work. As a decision to which they had all agreed, it encouraged all of them to write more purposefully than they might otherwise have done. We still used the maps.

My point, in summary, is this. We do well to itemise the menu on offer, in promoting literacy courses. But teachers are not the only cooks; literacy is about making, as well as consuming. We need help with the mixing and flavouring of the dishes. The principle of *inquiry* means that the teacher will continually be checking with the group as to their existing knowledge of these situations, and inviting them to contribute to and create the ingredients from which they may then create the course work. It also means that new items, not already known to be common, are given the space to emerge.

The à la carte menu offered in any course in communication skills, report writing or literacy/'Fresh start' might look like this:

writing letters
speaking up in meetings
dealing with forms
presenting your experience in interviews
writing reports and messages.

The reason these subjects are commonly found in courses of this kind is precisely because research and development work has suggested that they are literacy situations which commonly face a large number of people. There are certainly as many ways in which teachers then set about teaching these subjects as there are teachers. Still more variety (and relevance) is offered by a 'cafeteria' approach to language and literacy study – especially if it is cooked up by a group of students. If such a group has some experience in common – as would be the case with either a women-only group or a workplace training course – its members will, between them, be able to offer a series of situations which may be outside the experience of the teacher.

Here, for example, is a list of literacy tasks put together by a group of senior care staff working in residential homes for the elderly in 1990. They were attending a half-day course on 'report writing' as part of an in-service training programme. As their teacher, I needed to know what kinds of writing, including reports, they had to handle in the context of their jobs. They gave me examples. I asked them to give, for each, the content, audience and purpose. The list on the flipchart resulting from their examples looked like this:

What	About what	To whom	Why
List	Of residents' clothes	Another senior care officer	To check when she leaves
Report	Lady who had had a fall	Officer taking over	To tell officer – H&S file
Message	Resident gone out	Other staff on floor	To know where they are
Letter	Family	For resident's sister	Resident disabled
Letter	Accident	Hospital casualty officer	To tell them info. about patient
Request	Leave for holiday	Homes manager	To ask for permission
Report of incident	Something that you've witnessed	Homes manager	To get something done
Job appl.	Me and my skills; the job; equal opps	Soc. services	To get the job

Together, this list offers a curriculum for a whole course in workplace communication. A closer focus on the *content* of any one of these writing situations can also be approached in a similar way. (Later in this chapter I describe how another group, also working as care assistants in residential homes for the elderly, offered examples of the kind of report they might have to write in the daily report book about the individual residents they cared for.) My point is that this process is a research exercise for the students as much as the teacher: making visible the range of writing they already deal with affirms the literacy work they face on a daily basis, and provides material from which to pick out what kind of things they find difficult about it.

RESEARCHING THE ANSWERS

During the 1980s there were a number of new and stimulating debates about the nature of research in adult literacy. For those of us who teach, an immense body of thought from linguists, sociologists, anthropologists, historians and educational theorists became available to contribute to our own thinking. More significantly, some of these researchers set about making bridges with literacy teachers, partly as a result of those teachers themselves taking the step of undertaking academic research in some aspect of the work. Roz Ivanič's research work on punctuation, for example, 'started and ended with practical concerns'.[4] Similarly, six years of classroom experience and workshops preceded the publication of the Afro-Caribbean Language and Literacy Project's important set of ideas about language diversity.[5]

All this helped adult literacy work to mature from what has been called its 'activist phase'[6] of work to something more critical and reflective. Training for teachers has evolved to a stage when the 'self-questioning' attitude called for by one writer of that early phase[7] became regarded as a growing priority. The literacy worker, in the 1980s, was caught up in countless discussions (at conferences, in-service training courses, in newsletters and publications) as to the critical uses of literacy, her own literacy practice, and, above all, issues of language diversity, standard English and status.

During this period, however, the self-questioning teachers whom I talked with often conveyed a lack of confidence in their own capacities to theorise and research. The sheer everyday routines of fitting in teaching with all their other paid and unpaid responsibilities during the week made it hard to find the time or the circumstances in which to reflect on what they had seen and heard in the classroom. In this chapter, I am arguing that teachers, taking a research approach to the teaching, are already researchers; and that, by taking this approach, they offer an opportunity for their students to research and create new knowledge from their existing experience.

The teacher-researcher is a teacher open to surprises. She is also someone who recognises research as *planned learning*.[8] She is holding together the predictable with the unpredictable. Her job is to create an ambience in which all the participants are also willing to be open to surprise. To do this, she is there not to supply answers – for she has no ready-made ones – but to suggest alternatives; not to provide solutions, but to explore problems in a way in which solutions may emerge from others. As literacy detective, she encourages an investigative spirit in others.

By contrast, the teacher-instructor sees her purpose as to give instruction: to teach with answers. Part of her job, as she sees it, is to show students how to read and write better; to give rules, for example, in how spelling patterns work, and get them to practise these patterns. I suspect that most teachers, as I've said, place themselves somewhere between research and instruction; and many of us, in the space of a two-hour class, move several times between one and the other. Taken out of context, part of such a class might show any of us as good old-fashioned instructors. Such a scene features in the programme *Liberating literacy* (described in Chapter 1). We see a woman teacher in front of a class. She is dictating some words to illustrate a particular spelling pattern. She introduces the dictation by telling the class:

> *Ck* usually comes at the end of short words. Listen for it. We're going to try to spell some words today that end with *ck*. I'm going to read them out. You write them down. First word: *Lock*. Ready? Just as it sounds: *Lock*. [and so on, with other words].

She has begun with a 'rule'; she then offers a vocabulary list to practise it on. The choice of the vocabulary, as far as we can see from the film report, has been hers, rather than that of the students.

A teacher-researcher's strategy is to invite questions about spellings in the context of encouraging students to generate their own texts. In the process of these texts being written, a question may come up. This example took place in the context of a prison literacy class. We might well imagine, in this context, that one or more of the student writers in this class had wanted to write a sentence of their own which included the word 'lock' or 'locked up'. The student might have paused, and asked for help in spelling the word. At this stage the teacher might have simply to provide the correct spelling. Or she might have invited someone else in the group to offer it. They, and the student-writer who first asked, might then have been invited to think of any other words that might end the same way. The exercise we then see in this short film-clip could have emerged as a result of a process of research. The image of the instructing teacher is out of context, and we do not know.

A research approach to teaching rules and patterns about literacy often provides an answer that is better and more useful than the conventional one which the teacher might think of. Here are two examples that I have experienced:

1 In an evening literacy class: there was some discussion about the difference between reading and writing. 'What I can't understand', one student said, 'is why, if I can read it, I can't spell the word, when I come to write it.' I embarked on an explanation about the difference between the skills required of us in writing and those needed in reading. Then Maurice, another student, who had been listening, spoke. 'I think of it a bit like this', he said. 'If you were to ask me to draw a picture of my uncle, I couldn't do it. But if he were to walk into this room now, I could tell you that that man is my uncle. I would recognise him.' The explanation was far clearer than anything I had been trying to say: and thoroughly satisfied the other listeners.

2 In a daytime course on 'Improve your confidence in spelling': a woman asked what the rule was for the spelling pattern *ie*. In teacher-instructor mode, I answered with the formulation that I had myself been taught at school: '*i* before *e*, except after *c*'. The student said yes, she remembered being taught that rule, but it had never seemed to make sense to her. Another woman in the group joined in and agreed with her. She then said that she had worked out a different way of remembering this pattern. 'How I remember it,' she said, 'is like this: 'After *c* go *e*.' The first woman looked much more cheerful.

Both exchanges underlined for me the value of returning a question, directed at the teacher, to the group: and in the process, I had learned something new myself. Inviting other people to contribute their learning methods puts the teacher and the group in the position of continually researching new understandings of literacy issues.

WORDS AND CONTRADICTIONS

There is an idea that 'creative writing' belongs to playing rather than working. Sue Shrapnel Gardener described this view as one which,

> seems to put writing in a place that is at the same time special and useless. So we may think that it won't be suitable for all students, only the more 'advanced' or 'gifted' ones, and that there are other, more practical, kinds of writing on which we might more usefully spend our time.[9]

Taking inspiration from James Britton's work (which I referred to in chapter 2), she argued for a different perspective:

> 'If we need labels, I find more use in the division of writing into expressive, poetic and transactional writing (writing to make things happen)... This theory suggests we need a firm grip on the expressive before we tackle other uses of writing.

Most (but not all) of the items in the list of writing created by the senior care 'report writing' course group (p. 71) is a list of transactional writing. The writing was written for a purpose: to inform, to ask for permission, to put something on record (the H & S file – Health and Safety), to ask for action, to show support, to get a job. The one item in the list which is slightly different from this is the letter written for the resident to her sister. The purpose of giving information in this kind of writing is still here; but the audience is in a different relationship to the writer. She is writing on behalf of the resident, to someone the resident knows personally, her sister.

In order confidently to compose the sentences for a formal letter, report, message or job application, written to a reader in a less intimate relationship with the writer, any writer certainly needs a 'firm grip on the expressive'. It is interesting to note that sociolinguists studying children's writing development have argued that secondary schooling should do more to maintain primary school uses of 'the story', if younger students of literacy are to get a 'firm grip' on the range of writing they have to deal with in studying and employment situations. [10] By ensuring that writing in adult studies keeps encouraging stories – which might include (but do not always have to) writing about personal experience – the researching teacher encourages the idea of the researching student. Jane McLaughlin, writing about literacy education with multilingual students, has argued that story writing 'shows a student from the beginning that what they have to say is important, interesting and *worth writing down* – it is difficult enough sometimes to convince a native speaker of this, still more a speaker of another language'. In her experience, folk tales, as much as life experiences, can have this effect. She sees this as in opposition to a false division made between creative and functional writing, asserting instead that 'the "creative" work has many vital "functions"; and the "functional" work will be intrinsically involved with creativity'.[11]

In short, producing formal writing (such as reports and official letters) has a great deal to do with telling a good story. The oral work *is* work: it means telling the tale, and finding the words. In *Learning from experience* I suggested a method of encouraging student writing that includes 'assembling the vocabulary'. The process suggested is that of the 'brainstorm', and is one which is often called 'making the list'. It is a method recommended by teachers of adult creative writing classes.[12] It is an idea which, in my experience, is always productive in a group setting; and it demonstrates how a teacher committed to the research principle can encourage the idea of the researching student.

As an exercise for students to try out the idea of collecting words, I suggest a theme. The group is then invited to offer all the words they can think of associated with it. One example given in *Learning from experience* is that of ideas to do with the weather. There are of course numerous sub-themes to this. I suggest two exercises.

The first consists of cards, some blank, some written on. There are six keywords: dry, wet, light, dark, hot, cold. Other cards have words which may be associated with one of these words for example: dusty, moist, gleaming, shadowy, feverish, icy. I suggest that the group could use the cards as a game, to collect and add more words to each key word to make 'sets'. The second exercise consists of a sheet with words already written on them, and three columns at the bottom, headed 'wind', 'rain' and 'sun'. Students are invited to choose in which column to write the other words; these include 'damp', 'gentle', 'drenching', 'bright', 'biting', 'breezy' and so on.

For both these exercises, the teacher has already done some word collecting. What they intend to offer is a method which students could then use for their own themes and sub-themes. Unless a writing task is already imposed, most of us have to have some inspiration or theme in the first place. For this, I usually collect three or four short passages by a range of authors, which can offer ideas for style and form of work. (In the case of weather, I have used fiction and autobiography, tapes and transcripts of broadcast weather forecasts and/or weather reports from the press, and audio tape sound-effects of storms and rain.)

A development from this theme could be that of the elements: earth, air, fire and water. (In a four-day 'Linked learning' course for twenty-five women at Hillcroft College in 1985[13] this led to the group sharing stories of many moods – from seaside holidays to volcanoes, bonfires to hurricanes.)

This process of researching words is an important and enriching stage in a group of students seeking out both the subject and the vocabulary they want to write about; and it can be particularly useful as a way to explore conflicting feelings about themselves as adult learners. Many people think of themselves as slow at learning and poor at remembering what they have learned. It is no use the teacher dismissing these convictions as untrue. The students need space to explore how these ideas have come about. With a little cunning, however, they may also be persuaded of other truths about themselves. Invite them to talk to each other about how bad they are, or feel they are about their education: but ask them to spend equal time on something that they have learned successfully.

Two words with which I began such an exercise with the 1987 group were *slow* and *fast*. The aim was to open up the discussion about attitudes to learning and knowledge: the students' own, and other people's. I drew two columns on the flipchart, each headed by one of the words. I invited the group to associate any characteristic or mood that came to mind with these words. (Examples of words collected, by this and later groups, have been: *slow* – lazy, cautious, reserved, painstaking; *fast* – hasty, nimble, clever, speedy.)

On the table I put two piles of blank slips of paper, in two colours. The *slow* words were all written on the yellow slips (one word per slip); the *fast* words on the green slips. I invited students to pick out one word from each pile which they associated with themselves. They then talked to a partner about what this meant to them – and wrote a sentence or two for each of their words. Here are some of the writings that resulted that morning:

Vera (*speedy* and *lazy*).
When I go to work I am very speedy. Weekends I am lazy. When I go to work in the school I am speedy along the road. I am lazy at cooking, lazy at sewing, speedy at housework. I'm lazy at something because I don't like it. And I'm lazy at weekends because I'm wound up all the week!

Connie (*chatty* and *patient*).
I believe I am a very patient person. I don't get cross easily. I can't come into a room and just sort of talk to people. Some people can. I wish I could do that. But I am chatty with somebody I know well.

Margaret (*panicky* and *sleepy*).
When my son go out and don't return home early, I start to get panicky, and I keep saying, 'Where is he? God, I hope nothing happens to him.' When I have my work to do like washing clothes, I just leave it and go to sleep!

The value of the exercise in my experience is that it has the potential to release a lot of discussion about the values attached in competitive learning to *speed*. These women had spoken about themselves as 'slow' at learning and 'lazy' at writing. By inviting them to recall times when they thought it was important to be slow, painstaking and careful, they remembered the value they gave to their capacity for taking time – in being patient, for example, like Connie. As for *lazy* (a word conjuring up school reports and parents' judgements) Vera's comment about her 'laziness' speaks of two things: being lazy may be to do with being unmotivated; being lazy may simply mean being worn out.

In the previous chapter, I argued that respect should be given equally to both the uncertainties and to determination of adults looking to education as a path to change. Once they are students, those people also need to put in balance their feelings of doubt about their literacy with their feelings of power in other situations. Another exercise (that I used with the 1987 group and many times since), which provides a way for a group to hold together opposite feelings, is one that begins with these two phrases:

'I want to learn/have always wanted to learn . . .'; and 'I am good at . . . '

For this, students work in pairs, asking their partner to complete both statements in conversation. From this talk, they each then draft two sentences, each starting with one of the two phrases. It is important to insist that the discussion gives equal time to both statements. Women, especially, will have plenty to say about the first, and may only complete the second with one or two words ('I am good at cooking'). The rule for the exercise is to require the partner to push the speaker into saying more ('What kind of cooking?').

Here, from another group, are two pairs of statements they produced from this activity:

Rosemarie: I would like to learn how to write a letter. I would also like to learn how to spell and read. I am very interested in learning about people in the past who lived in Britain. I have a tremendous fear of reading, writing and spelling.

I am good at swimming. I go twice a week. I am also good at sewing. I began sewing at school and at the moment I am making covers for my brother's caravan.

Betty: I want to learn how to spell and put words together. I am good at making clothes and looking after children. I am also good at my job, most of all caring for old people.

These statements take a couple of minutes to read. But the discussion which preceded them took twenty. Much of what was said did not, of course, get written down. But the talk – and the persuasive listener, in each case – had encouraged some writing.

Literacy education, I suggested earlier, is built on paradox. This is possibly because most people, if we stop and think about it, are made up of paradoxes. Fear and hope, pride and uncertainty, coexist and alternate. In the same way, as I suggested earlier, those of us who are teachers sometimes move back and forth from being an 'instructor' to being a 'researcher'. Researching and sharing some of these contradictions in a group reveals, not only more about the individuals' diversity of knowledge and skills, but also some common themes for development later. These are not mutually exclusive oppositions: they exist together. In the same way, I suggest, this approach brings together the apparent opposition of what is 'creative' and what is 'functional' literacy, which, as Jane McLaughlin argued, are in any case interchangeable.

Earlier, I listed some situations generated by a group of senior care assistants working in residential homes for the elderly. Another group, also care assistants, told me about the kinds of situations which they might be asked to record in the daily report book. They spoke of the elderly individuals in their care. They capped one anecdote with another, across the table. The reports they had to write in the book were short – one-liners mostly – for the record, and for the next shift to read. The problem for the people in this group was that some of the vocabulary they would have to use they would find hard to spell. So, with their help, I wrote some of the kinds of sentences they would have to write. Together, we marked the words they found hard to spell, and now wanted to notice and practise. The exercise produced a text, then, for functional purposes. But the activity of producing it was without question a creative one. These were some of the sentences they produced:

Mr Mitchell seems to have an infection in his urine.
The rash on Mrs Wood's groin appears to be inflamed.
Mary More had a fall and bruised her hip.
Mrs Simpson's urine was discoloured and smelt offensive.
Mrs Jones has a rash on her face which seems to irritate her.

No amount of advance planning on my part could have told me that this was the text this group would want to work on. Until I had met with staff who work with frail and sometimes confused elderly people, it had been outside my experience. As I suggested earlier, the inquiry principle keeps the students at the centre of the curriculum, as people with experiences which the teacher cannot have had. The menu of literacy situations on which they may practise and develop their literacy confidence is a menu of which they have specialist knowledge; and the process of discussion in which group members themselves propose the written work has its own value. It is a process which enables students to relive and retell the situations and contexts in which the reading and writing takes place.

The relationship between the uses made of literacy in everyday life and the moments of concentrated thinking and talk in a classroom on the same subject is an important one. The activity of learning engaged in by students and educators adopting the principle of inquiry is – despite teachers' frequent sense of isolation in the process – a research activity. At the first national conference addressing the relationship between research and practice in adult literacy in 1984, there was 'a great eagerness to build on, and get recognition for, the embryonic research activities that grow naturally from everyday teaching and learning'.[14] That eagerness has, since then, grown and thrived in the form of a national network known as RaPAL (Research and Practice in Adult Literacy), and undoubtedly provided an important and mutually supportive forum for adult literacy education.

Adult education classes can sometimes feel like blessed islands – away from outside pressures to compete and pass tests. They are themselves, however, a context with its own pressures. In the next chapter I relate the general atmosphere of an inquiring group to what I see as a central principle in literacy education: namely, that a reader or writer's belief in their own *authorship* gives new strength to both their reading and writing.

5

AUTHORS AND IDENTITY

In this chapter I focus on the principle of *authorship* in literacy work. That is, a use of literacy in which the student comes to own the text in front of them: it is theirs.

As I suggested in the Introduction, the experience I have learned from has led me to a preoccupation with making explicit the rationale behind the methods we propose to students for developing their literacy. Rightly, teachers have also been concerned to ensure that students, too, take responsibility for deciding what and how they choose to learn. Most adult literacy teachers, being part-time, are only too aware of the limits of time they and their students have. People who join literacy classes, as students or teachers, have enormous other lives to lead, huge responsibilities and hopes and fears of other kinds, and vast stores of history and knowledge to draw on. This little time we have together, a few hours a week, is time which students have given voluntarily, with no insurance that it is worth the other things they could have been doing instead, and with every possibility that it could be boring, damaging or wasteful. As teachers of literacy, we owe them explicit statements of purpose, at every stage in the teaching process.

Students, in short, deserve our honesty, and are entitled to have answers to the key question – why are you asking me to do this? – even if they are too polite to ask it. In the previous two chapters I described something of what educators stand to gain from encouraging the sometimes difficult questions about literacy. Here, my concern is with restating to students the principle of *authorship*: namely, that in order for any of us to believe ourselves literate (and literacy is in large part a matter of belief) we need to recognise ourselves as writers – as authors of our own words. If this principle is made explicit, then educators and students together recognise, also, that time taken in discussion of writing – their own and other people's – is purposeful time.

A writer writes, first, for herself. For this reason I begin with a section on private writing, and the move student writers can make from private to public, illustrating this with three case studies. Second, I discuss the rights and responsibilities of writers, and describe a way in which the principle of authorship can be experienced in a classroom where all participants, students and teacher, write to each other. Third, I offer examples of inspirations to authorship which relate verbal and visual expression.

FROM PRIVATE TO PUBLIC

There are several teaching ideas I described in *Learning from experience* that I have changed, or not used since then; but I was surprised to note, rereading it ten years on, that there are a majority of them that I have continued to use, add to and develop. The key purpose of this book, as I have said, is not to discuss how these or any other ideas may be useful in promoting and encouraging literacy development, but to examine *why* they may be so. Here, I pick out three of them in order to illustrate the *authorship* principle: (i) the diary, (ii) the group word poem, and (iii) the description of 'a person I know' (originally, 'a place I know'). (In chapters 6 and 7 I pick out others, also developed from *Learning from experience*. I have not chosen to illustrate principles from other people's teaching ideas because I have less experience of these; although undoubtedly mine have been influenced by countless good ideas over the years, shared by colleagues, in handbooks and seminars.) In each case, and throughout the book, I also try to clarify what can be said to justify, to the students, this use of their time rather than any other.

Private writing is always a good place both to start and to return to. In practice, the public showing of writing, to which I will refer later, continually interweaves with this hidden work. We write first for ourselves; and the concept of rough drafts, which literacy teachers regularly propose to their students, concerns an essentially private, experimental concept of writing. (It doesn't have to be right the first time. Write it rough, cross it out, everyone does it.) In the case of the 'diary sheet' which I offered in *Learning from experience*, I have been told by teachers over the years that this exercise has often provided a means for students to make for themselves the link between the private and the public. The idea proposed is that everyone (including the tutor(s)) has a copy of the same A4 sheet, divided up into the seven days; everyone undertakes to write something in each of the seven spaces – however apparently trivial; and in class, the following week, students and teacher(s) read out, or show each other, or simply talk from the diary pages they have used.

Diaries are a chosen habit. It is important that the invitation to a group to take away diary sheets and write something short for each day remains that – an invitation. It is a kind of voluntary homework; but its value is lost if it becomes regularly 'imposed' as a weekly chore.[1] Students must decide for themselves, from trying out the habit, what its values and pleasures are. Since few people write daily as a habit, it is for many a new experience; and it is in adult literacy education that they first discover the practice of 'keeping a diary'. I have heard a number of students express surprise at the pleasure of doing so. As to why it is a practice worth recommending, it is always worth saying the obvious: that anyone wishing to improve and develop their writing will do so by practice, and that diary writing provides a structure of writing short pieces which can (but don't have to be) produced every day. It is also important to say that there are no rules as to what to write, except to write something, and that no two people will write diary entries in the same way. The pleasure of writing a diary is a freedom from writing conventions. There is no right way to write a diary.

Students who do not write a diary, following the invitation to bring it in to next week's class, say one of two things: 'I didn't have time', or 'I didn't do anything worth writing about'. Persuaded into it with the argument about practice and improvement, those unwilling writers may, for the following week, limit their entries to the 'Got up. Went to work. Got home, had tea, watched TV' variety; or, 'It is my wife's birthday'. This, for many students, is an enormous move forward and should be recognised as such. They are composing original prose.

The move from this kind of writing to something a little more adventurous may come after voicing complaints, as one student did, that his diary (and his life) was 'boring'. Noticing how other people spoke about their diaries, or read from them in the literacy class, and encouraged, despite himself, by other students' disagreeing with his self-criticism, he picked up ideas – as an author – for other things he could write about: the people he had seen at the bus stop, the progress of a cupboard he was making, a sentence his child had uttered. This noticing, however, has to be deliberately encouraged. In a group, in which several people have brought in a diary sheet, the tutor invites anyone willing to do so to read out part of what they have written. She could do this by asking 'What did anyone write for last Saturday?' and five or six different Saturdays are read and listened to. As in every case when a group shares their own writing in this way, it is always important to pause after each and invite responses and questions. The author is in the room: the opportunity is there for her or his readers to show interest and questioning towards their writing. (I say more about how this exchange between reading and writing readers in the group can encourage development of the writing in the next chapter.)

The first reader of the diary is the author.[2] The author, in this case, deciding he wanted something more interesting to read, began to write more interesting sentences – encouraged, by the discussion in the class about other people's diaries, to ignore, for the time being, his frustration with spelling.

The 'group poem' idea suggested in *Learning from experience* was based on using the framework of 26 lines, each starting with a letter of the alphabet, to write thoughts on a particular theme. The 'alphabet poem' has been much in evidence in student magazines from literacy classes in the last ten years. I have found it a useful framework myself in which to work with a group. The idea was a simple one: take a theme, take the alphabet, and, as a group, find a way, by using the initial letters, of expressing the theme as a poem. The only rule was that there should be no requirement to rhyme. (The alphabet is written up vertically on a large sheet of paper which everyone can see. Offers of words or phrases using any initial letter are invited – starting anywhere. No need to start with A. Poems have been written on work, on school memories, on health, on music and so on.)

A variant on this, is simply to start with an idea and use the word-association approach to develop a poem – either sticking with the idea, or allowing one word or phrase to suggest another, developing the theme into others. The method is the same: use a large sheet of paper, visible to everyone; invite contributions from the whole group; discuss, as a group, what to write and what not to write. The teacher acts as group scribe, asking for guidance as to where to begin lines, how to lay it out, and what to put down. The same rule – freedom from rhyme – is vital: but the same idea of a poem, free of requirements to punctuate or complete sentences, is central. Its purpose, within the principle of authorship, is, this time, for a group to recognise its powers as a collective author. Its use, in writing and literacy groups which may have reached a moment of pause in other work, is to offer a creative exercise which provides an immediate result (group poems I have done have occupied between 5–20 minutes of a group's time).

The following poem was the result of five students working with me in a session on writing during an in-service course for Lewisham Council clerical staff on 'women and management' in 1990. I had suggested it as a humorous relief for a group of mature women whose discussion about work responsibilities had included references to frustration and stress. As a way out, for the last ten minutes of class time, I asked them to talk about what they remembered about their dreams of life now when they had been children. Actually, the written result from the process was only partly light-hearted. Hopes and realities collide in a short space. We called the poem, 'When I grow up'. This is it:

> *When I grow up*
> Facing harsh realities
>   the buck stops
>   with you;
>   expectations
>
> 'When I grow up I'll be free'
> When I grow up I want to be
>   rich
>   comfortable
>   free from strain
>
> When I grow up I'll have the choice
> to do cake decorating,
> hang gliding,
> reading books
>   for pleasure
>
> When I grow up
> I'll look after my grandmother
> for ever;
>   she's calm
>   talks with her eyes,
>   wisely

As I grow up, I've got
   more worries;
   I think – 'I've never been depressed before;
   but now I've got the pressure';
   I have to cope, and be hurt.

Leaving home.
Growing up.[3]

Third, the description of 'a person I know'. This exercise, originally 'a place I know' in *Learning from experience*, was illustrated by several extracts from other published writers. The idea was to encourage students, inspired by these, to write their own. I have often used this theme since; but I have also used, more often, the subject of 'someone I know'. There are three good things about it. First, since many people's writing purposes include writing reports about other people, this subject has a relevance to their immediate literacy interests which is not always apparent in other writing topics. Second, it is my experience that, for students at any level of literacy education, writing about someone else is often more attractive than writing about themselves. There is genuine interest in recalling to mind a familiar person and trying to find the means to describe them for someone who does not know them. And third, the interest expressed in both the person and the description offered by others in the group when the writing is shared can provide a double affirmation to a writer who finds other writing subjects less easy to handle – affirmation both of her capacity to write, and of her knowledge of the person she describes. She has conjured up another person in the room.

In a sense, however, this subject returns us to the 'problems of representation' discussed in chapter 1. Any of us trying to describe someone we know faces a problem when we try to bring them to life for someone who has never met them. This is why it is useful to begin the exercise with dialogue. The following account of one group's work with it suggests how this talk and writing worked together.

In 1991 I taught two courses for care assistants in Lewisham Council. The courses were called 'Improve your confidence in spelling'. Twelve people came to each course. The course ran every Wednesday from 9.30 to 4.0 (with lunch break) for five weeks. After the first week, the students agreed to do the diary exercise for the following week. The second week's 'assignment' was to write something about someone they knew. I suggested they could write about one of the elderly residents in the homes where they worked – a neighbour, or a friend – and to imagine that the person reading it had never met the person.

To make it possible for them to write something at home, I discussed the subject with them first, then asked them to work in pairs. One person was to act as secretary and listener to the other, asking them about the person they were going to write about, and trying to write down odd words which the speaker could later use as notes for the writing they would do. Then they reversed roles.

Using the talk and the notes, everyone wrote something at home. Several students spoke with surprise, later, not only at how much they had managed to write (having at first thought, at the prospect of it, that they would have little to say) but also, importantly, at how they had actually enjoyed writing it.

The work of the class was then to read, respond to and complete these drafts. I must also confess that, when I asked if they wanted me, as teacher, to read them individually and offer written comments, there was a unanimous 'yes' from both course groups. Having resisted the teacher-marked essay in years of literacy work, there are times like this when you have to give in. My own strategy – and every literacy teacher has her own way of dealing with this – is to avoid making any marks on the original writing. At most, I make a mark in the margin and a circle round the word I am picking out for comment. At the end of the piece, I write a note to the author offering recognition to the content of the work, list the words I have marked, and ask them to find them on their text and correct them from these. I don't believe this strategy is the best; but it is the one I have found which remains most consistent with the principles of authorship and equality.

When the authors got these back, they did their own 'proof-reading', and read each others' pieces. Finally, at the end of the course, I asked if they wanted any of the coursework that they had done typed and collated as a course 'souvenir'. Again, the answer was 'yes'. All the four examples I now offer are therefore, in all senses, from published writing (we printed 25 copies of each course magazine).

My school friend. Debra's handwritten copy of this, now, on my desk, recalls her face and voice to me as no typed copy ever could. There are several overwritten words from her corrections to the

89

spelling. The writing is round and cursive. This is what she wrote:

> The name of my school friend is Jean. Jean and myself grew up together from a very young age. We both attended the same infant school, before we started elementary school.
>
> Jean was a very intelligent girl and had a lovely voice. Jean was always happy. There was never a dull moment for her. Dancing was her greatest gift. At school she performed concerts and the other kids would gather around to listen to her. She was always top of the class. Jean attended Sunday school, and when it was time for singing her voice was heard above everyone else's.
>
> Jean left elementary school and attended secondary and I went on to another school. Once our schooling was over, Jean came to England, got married and went to live in Birmingham. Two years later I came to England and got married.
>
> Jean still lives in Birmingham but we still keep in contact with each other. Although many years have passed, I still see her as a close friend. I value her friendship as she is very special to me.

This is a piece of writing that encompasses, in four paragraphs, thirty years.

Mrs Ezra. Pat wrote this by dictation. This was her first experience of an adult literacy class, and only her second week in this course. When I typed it for the course magazine, I laid it out in sentence and meaning units, with the idea that she could reread it with more ease.

> Mrs Ezra is a very loving person.
> She lives in a complete world of her own.
> The care assistants get her up in the morning and wash and dress her for the day.
> The care assistants take her to the alcove where Mrs Ezra sits all day.
> She is taken from there for her meals.
> The beautiful old lady sits and mutters to herself all day long.
> All she says is 'Ma ma ma'.
> Mrs Ezra does not watch any television.
> She is so lonely.
> But the care assistants cheer her up by talking to her.

The original text was in the handwriting of my co-tutor, Iiola: but the author is Pat, who registered delight when the group listened to Iiola first read it out to the group (some of whom had also met Mrs Ezra, and enjoyed Pat's feeling for her). It was the first time that Pat had seen a piece of continuous prose on paper that was her own work – rather than copy writing. It was also the first time she had seen others appreciate her as an author. (At the time of writing, four months later, Pat is attending regularly a local literacy class and composing writing independently of a scribe.)

My neighbour. Agnes chose to talk, and then write, about her neighbour.

> When my neighbour Clare moved in next door to me I was a bit apprehensive. It took me a long time before we started talking to each other. I hardly see her. She was very shy. One day I decided to knock at her door to introduce myself.
>
> I found out Clare is a very loving and caring person. She has three children, two boys and one girl. Her children are kind and helpful, always willing to help. If someone comes to visit me while I was out Clare would invite them into her house and give them a cup of tea. Clare looks after my granddaughter while my daughter-in-law is in college.
>
> Myself and Clare became good friends. When the weather is nice we sit out in the garden and talk. I would like to take Clare on a nice holiday.

When she was writing, Agnes knew the kind of word she wanted, at the end of her first sentence, but she asked for ideas from me and others before she chose 'apprehensive' – and then needed to check its spelling. That's what authorship means: choosing exactly what you want to say, rather than finding a word that will do as second-best.

Phyllis. Andrea's first language is Italian. She speaks English fluently, but worries that her written English is not always correct. In this piece, writing about a resident she knew well, she had trouble, not with her English, but with clarifying what she knew but I didn't. In her first draft, she had written at the beginning of the second paragraph simply that 'This lady is very difficult to understand when you first get her up'. My questions as to why she was more difficult then than at any other time of the day led to her explanatory phrase which she then added, 'until she has her medication', and to the examples, not only of the difficulty of understanding her, but also the difficulty of being patient:

> Phyllis suffers from Parkinsons disease. She is incontinent at night only and tends to worry a lot about any changes. She has been at this home about six years. She has no children; her husband was from Jersey and she speaks of him with much affection; she has a nephew who visits her every Friday and brings her fruit and sweets.
>
> This lady is very difficult to understand when you first get her up. Until she has her medication her speech is not clear; she can be very trying as she keeps telling you what to do next for her. You're putting her vest on and she says 'Please help me put on my petticoat'; You haven't finished that and she wants the next garment. You've got her dentures in your hand and she says 'Please put my teeth in'. It's non-stop.
>
> But after breakfast when she has taken her medication, she's able to walk with her zimmer and be self-caring for the rest of the day.
>
> Phyllis enjoys a conversation and is good at remembering what we talked about and names of members of my family. She has a daily paper and talks about world affairs and seems concerned and sad about other people's sufferings.
>
> She likes her hair to look nice and has it set every two weeks. She also enjoys her weekly bath.
>
> Phyllis has formed a few friends with the residents and staff. George, one of the residents, sits in the lounge for his meals and Phyllis likes to shake hands with him and have a few words when she passes him. She became very concerned when he went into hospital for a few days.
>
> The one thing Phyllis often says to me is, 'I never thought I would end up like this and in a home. I was always very active sewing, knitting, crocheting and so on, and I had a good home.'

Your reaction as reader to these printed passages may well be something like this: are these all, strictly, literacy students? Surely these are all, except Pat's perhaps, writings from confident writers? My answer is to restate the case: literacy education extends beyond reading texts by unknown authors; it concerns the complex work of authors making their own texts. All the students on these two courses were people who had defined themselves as wanting to 'improve' their literacy. The keyword in the course title, as I discussed with them, was the word 'confidence': they were there to improve their 'confidence in spelling'. (Other work we did during the course is discussed in chapter 3.) All these women, from the five days I spent with them, referred to themselves as 'bad at' writing, and in particular, 'bad at' spelling. So, yes, all these texts, in their original, had spelling mistakes in them; all, in this sense, were the work of literacy students. Andrea left out speech marks (or apostrophes) in the quoted speech of Phyllis. Debra confused commas and full stops. Agnes put in capital letters in the middle of sentences but not always at their beginnings. All of them had words they misspelt. None of this is as important as the fact that every one of these and the other course participants wrote their own pieces, found, for the time being, their own ways of writing, and took responsibility for being published. Correcting mistakes is a small part of literacy education. This other work is its central business.

'Writing', as John Richmond has put it, 'is a profoundly creative activity.' 'It is an obvious but still striking fact that every day people compose and write down texts which have never been written down before.'[4] For each of the authors just quoted, as for anyone sitting down to write, there is no certainty as to what is about to happen. Nobody had ever written what they were about to write: in front of them, they now had something they had made themselves. Adult literacy work in this country has often, and rightly, tried to identify for itself a very different role than that of schooling. Our students' recalled school histories have told us often enough that our job is to provide something different, more liberating and less punitive. It has, however, been equally important (as Nell Keddie[5] and Sue Shrapnel Gardener[6] have argued in different ways), to recognise the extent of common ground between English curriculum policies in schools and literacy and communication skills curricula in adult and further education. Richmond, in addressing school teachers, could equally be addressing a training course for adult education tutors, when he urges them to encourage publication of their pupils' writing (starting with what he delightfully calls 'the classroom community' itself):

> Publication should be simple and frequent. Regular occasions when children read their writing to the class; a stout folder containing plastic transparent loose leaves, where recently produced writing, in original or photocopy, from as many

writers in the class as possible and preferably from everybody, can be read; extensive use of the display board; booklets by individual authors, illustrated and with a cover; the best of the writing (placing a highly relative emphasis on 'best' to be typed and printed in editions of 50 or 100 or 200, to become part of the class's and the school's reading.[7]

Even with the contraints on resources and funding, most of these methods are still available to basic education and 'return to study' courses (always supposing the photocopier is still working).

RIGHTS AND RESPONSIBILITIES

Authors have, like other people, both rights and responsibilities. We have the right to find our own way of expressing something; we also have to take responsibility for the writing being ours. Having said this, no author is free of other people; and in literacy work in groups, the process both of finding our voice and of becoming publicly accountable for our writing embraces many possibilities of inspiration, guidance, support and criticism from others. In short, literacy students, working in a group, arrive at authorship with multiple sources of help; but they arrive there in their own right.

Putting pen to paper and starting a sentence with the words 'I am' is not easy. We start writing: 'I live', 'I have', 'I like', and wonder what to say next.[8] Writing a complete sentence with these beginnings, however, enables us to see something of ourselves on paper: our present becomes our past; what is inside our head becomes outside, visible and detached from us. Every time we write an application for a job we call on these phrases and others; and we ask our students to do the same, thinking it ordinary. And indeed they are ordinary, aren't they? After all, they are phrases in everyday conversational use.

However, as I suggested in chapter 2, there is an important difference between saying 'I am Hyacinth Roberts' or 'I like going to church' and writing these sentences on paper. The spoken words are gone; the writing is there and can be reread. That gives us both more power and less control. Once it is passed on to someone who does not know us, we are exposed to the possibility of questions. In short, we might have it wrong: both the spelling and the statement await judgement. (The courtroom looms: Are you sure that's how you spell Roberts? Are you sure you are not *Hilary* Roberts?)

Writing, as I discussed in the last section, makes us public – and, once the writing leaves our hands, published. And in a literacy classroom, the sense of *being published* is as acute for a new writer passing her writing across the table to another person (whether that person be her peer, a student, or the person she sees in authority, the teacher) as it is for anyone awaiting reaction from a published article or book. In some ways, the sense of anxiety is much keener: the reader is before her, while the reader of the journal or book is usually at a safe distance, out of sight. She waits for their reaction. They look up and say 'I like it, it's good', and her face shows a mixture of relief and disbelief.[9] Having seen this happen in many different groups, it's been my feeling for a long time that 'published writing' and 'published authors' are concepts which deserve broader definition than the usual. I suggest: published writing is public writing; public writing is writing we let go to a reader unknown to us.

If we are convinced, as literacy teachers, that literacy is worth the effort, then we must also, in my view, see it as our job to demonstrate that conviction. There are two ways we can do this. One is to remain in touch, through our own uses of literacy, with the struggle and moments of happiness which these give us. The second is to offer our own writing and reading experience as part of the class material. By this I don't mean inflicting our poetry on our students, or showing off our latest formal letter or report. I mean that inviting our students to see themselves as authors, who belong to a community of other authors means sharing by example our own struggles with reading and with writing. Certainly, it's usual for a teacher in a literacy class to write words – her own or other people's – on the flipchart or board; the suggestion here is that sometimes, at the moment when students are writing at her encouragement, she could sit beside them and write, too. This act ensures that the moment of composing is genuinely the creative space for writing that she has tried to say it is: the critic, waiting in the wings to spring on the next sentence (or gently suggest a correction to the last one), is banished from the room.[10]

A common enough situation in literacy classes is the moment when a new student arrives in the class, half an hour into class time. She had an appointment an hour earlier, but her babysitter was late and she missed the bus. What's to be done? How can she be put at ease? Another student may be willing to break off from what they are doing to talk to her. You may sit with her for a few minutes, learn her name, tell her yours, explain something of what is going on. The question in your mind, as teacher, is how do you find out her literacy level, needs and interests, and at the same time introduce her to how the class works?

An example of the teacher-writer position that I am proposing is the following solution to this dilemma. Agree that you write each other a letter, there and then. Explain you will write to her, and she writes to you. Offer her the spelling of your name; check you can spell hers. Say there is no rule or test, only that the letter begins 'Dear – '. Suggest she tells you something about herself and why she has come. Then you both start writing. She may get stuck; so may you. Stop and talk about it. Find out what's holding her up: the spelling? What to say next? And tell her about what's holding you up. After a few minutes, when you've both got as far as you can, agree to end. You may want to discuss the appropriate words you want to end with ('Best wishes, Jane' are the ones I usually use).

She now has something of you to read. You have something of her. It's a start: an introduction to who you each are, and to two of the key principles on which you try to run the class; authorship, and equality.

She is learning that she has an equal right to respect for what she has written; and that she has an equal share of responsibility for deciding how she can write it. (Authorship, understood in a more public sense, is sometimes associated with another responsibility: namely, a 'responsibility to the readers'. All sorts of alarming things seem to be implied by such a phrase: a responsibility to be intelligible, truthful, accurate, and so on. For this reason, the emphasis here being on *draft writing*, with a known and present reader, I have left this weighty question to the next chapter, where it can be understood as part of the principle of *equality* between readers and writers.)

INSPIRATIONS

After courses end, correspondence can begin. I wish this happened more often, but letter-writing between students who have shared a course does not in my experience seem to be a common practice. (Letters from one course or centre to another, however – 'a pen pal scheme' – has often featured in creative literacy work.)[11] One letter can 'inspire' another. After the end of the 'Fresh start' course I described in chapter 4, students did for a short time write to each other, and to me. This is one letter that I have kept and reread, from a student called Amy (reproduced here as she wrote it):

> 'Dear Jane,
> It's been a Pleasure to know you With this few lines, you will learn that your letter I have received safely, and was indeed, glad to here from you.
>
> Well as I told you before I am very lazy to write I miss the Girls very much, I won't be writing one but you and I'm making A Big Effort to do so, I'm enjoying the sun shine, I know it won't be for long, but thats life I am expecting my Brother and his wife 7 Aug so I'll be very Busy for the next few weeks. I do hope you can read my writing.
>
> Well Jane I started to write this letter since 3 of August and started to sleep so I put it Aside and forget all about it, then my Brother and his wife arrived on the 7 of August and that was it, Anyway better late than Never I do hope Ill be able to come 23 Sept
> Best wishes,
> Amy.

The letter is dated 2 September; and I felt moved that Amy not only started it, but finished it (after a gap of a month between paragraphs two and three) – and sent it. Her writing on the course had inspired me to write to her; reading that letter had had the same effect and inspired her to write to me. We each had a known reader.

A lot of teachers use pictures in literacy work. A good friend, one night when I was panicked at the prospect of the new literacy course I was starting the next day, gave me a piece of simple advice. I had prepared and over-prepared all the things I intended to do in the first session. But I could not think of a warm-up exercise after the introduction. 'Take a bunch of old postcards,' she said. 'Any will do. Cut some pictures out of magazines. Just a dozen or so is all you need. Take them in, give them one each, and get them to talk to each other in pairs about their picture for five minutes.' [12]

With variations, I have used the exercise many times since. Sometimes I have asked students to hide their picture from their partner, and to try to give them in words everything the picture shows them. Then the partner looks at the picture and says in what ways their image of it was different. The purpose of the exercise – which needs to be made clear at the outset – is not to test what the picture-describer left out, but to discuss on equal terms some of the issues of reporting on what we observe. What one person sees first, the second may notice last. This is not wrong, or right: it is about different perceptions of the same thing.

I have co-taught three courses using photography and writing, and more recently three one-day workshops on television, talk and writing. In all cases, the primary interest of participants was to 'improve' their literacy. We knew it would be difficult to attract students to the photography/writing courses: and it was. They were either already attending a literacy class, or they weren't clear how photography would help them with their spelling and reading. We designed the first courses to last five sessions over five weeks, and hoped to encourage people by choosing 'Making a book' as the course title and purpose: the students would talk about and then make, by the end of the course, their own book of photographs and text. The first course had a group of five students; the second, six. The third course ran for ten weeks, with a group of eight students. In the 'Television, talk and writing' days, the story was different. We were fortunate to have the help of three different local literacy organisers to do the job of publicising and enrolling students for three Saturday events. An average of seventeen students came to each of these. At these events (by contrast with the photography courses and any usual literacy class), almost no writing was done during the day: the focus of the work was discussion, viewing clips of television programmes, and more discussion.[13]

Both these sets of experiences taught me a lot about using imagery in literacy work. Reading pictures – still or moving – and reading words on a page ask of us similar uses of memory, imagination and analysis: we have to make our own meanings, rarely the same as other people's, of what we see.

The two groups from the 'Making a book' courses did make their own books: using us, the two tutors, as darkroom processor and typist for the photographs and writing they did. While I would not want to make any special claims as to the change in confidence or literacy skills that resulted for the course participants, I think there were two important aspects of reading and writing which these courses addressed more explicitly than is often the case in literacy work: namely the *content*, and *form* of published books. In each case, the group became during the five weeks a group of authors: starting, editing and finishing their writing within the period of the course. They had in common an editorial theme: that of hands. This was an imposed theme, since we, the tutors, had defined it on the first day as the subject both of the photography and the writing. Within the boundaries of the subject, however, the writers made their own statements and choices, and generated the content of their own published collection.

As to the question of *form*, the group spent two of the five sessions comparing and discussing the form and design of a random selection of other books spread out on the table, and the parts of the remaining three sessions making decisions about the look of the publication they wanted theirs to be. We discussed questions about the *structure* of books: contents pages, cover design, titles, relationship between image and text and layout of print. What attracts us to pick up any publication? What helps us choose what to read? If we are to address the issue of students' own authorship, discussion of this kind has a particular importance. For any group which includes people who find reading hard, or who even say 'I can't read at all', there is a release of energy to be found from an open discussion which looks at published books, not as inaccessible sources of authority, but as objects which may or may not attract any of us.

Here are three short examples of the picture/writing work done during this process. All three are copied from the final, fair copy that each author had made after their first draft, with spellings corrected by them, with help. In the process of writing them, as I try to indicate, new inspirations helped the writer overcome hesitation.

1 A picture taken by another student, of a third. The writer picks it off the pile, and decides that is the picture she will write about. The picture taken shows Mary using her hands to hold a phone. The writer writes: 'Mary is working in an office. She is on the phone and she is holding on to a pen.' *(Pause. What else can I say? she asks me. Imagine, I say. What do you think Mary is doing, or might be doing?)* 'And she is holding on to a pen – and is writing out an order which has come through from someone.' *(Second pause. The writer looks again at the picture, at the expression on Mary's face, and adds:)* 'Quietly she listens to what was being said at the other end.'

2 A picture of the author, taken by another student. He chooses to write this about it: 'This picture shows me winding my watch. I quite often forget to wind it up and it stops going.' *(I'm stuck, he says. What else do you want me to say? Students often ask teachers 'what do you want me to write/say?' The teacher's job,*

here as at every other point, is to give them the rights and the responsibility of authorship. Where did you get it? I asked. Oh alright, I'll write about that, he says.) 'I got the watch in a shop in the West End. The strap was not on it as the old one was made of plastic. The strap on it now I made myself some time ago.' *(Another student has a look at what he is writing. Looks at the watch he is wearing, in real life, more closely. They get into conversation about it. Eventually they separate, to add a bit more to their writing. This author, as a result of the conversation has thought of more things he could add, and writes:)* 'My watch is very big and feels heavy sometimes. The strap on it now is made of leather and took me quite a few weeks to get it right.'

3 A third picture, taken by the author, of me. This time the hands are tying the shoelace. She picks this picture out of the pile. Her first four sentences are an introduction with a strong sense of a reader: 'I am Hyacinth Roberts. We meet every Wednesday morning at the Lee Centre. Coming here makes me feel warm inside. I am the one who takes this picture, with my Jane tying her shoe lace.' *(The next four are different. It's as if she is stuck, but is keeping going anyway with something she feels she ought to write.)* 'I hope this picture will teach us how important our hands are. What would we do without our hands? Without our hands we couldn't feel ourselves, comb our hair, even have a bath, etc. I believe the most important members of our body is our hands.' *(Someone comes to read what she has written. They look at her picture again. They talk about tying shoelaces, memories. Hyacinth reads what they have written about another picture. She returns to her own writing and says more:)* 'Remembering when I was a child it was very hard learning to tie shoe laces. Sometimes I even tie it on the side of my shoe. Anyway in the end I did learn to tie my shoe lace. The problem was not using my hands properly. It's different now I learn it all.'

How are we to judge this process? and how do we assess these pieces of writing? In the first two sections of this chapter I discussed the relationship between individual, private writing and writing like this, written in a group, put together as a group. My own assessment is that each of these three examples of writing processes illustrates different approaches to the principle of authorship within 'the classroom community'. In (1) the picture chosen was taken by another, and showed a third person. The writer was reporter – but also imaginative storyteller ('quietly she listens'). In (2), the picture is of the author, taken by someone else. Again, he reports – but this time, as autobiographer: after the first sentence, every line tells us something about him. Example (3) is written by the photographer herself: reporting again, this time on the context of the picture, then on what she sees to be its didactic purpose, and lastly on its association for her. These three people took on the job of authorship on the basis of three different sets of choices. In order to assess the quality of their work as writing – as literature – we must recognise its genesis, and remember the first principle discussed in this book: the principle of context.

6

READERS EQUAL WRITERS

Inequality: in literacy there's plenty of it about. Unequal status given
to different kinds of English; unequal attention to other languages
than English; unequal relationships between people called 'writers'
and the rest, the readers. This chapter focuses chiefly on this third
inequality, and how to address it. The inspiration for it came from a
woman literacy student I interviewed many years ago who said, as
she was leaving the interview: 'I don't want to be greedy: I just want
to read what's on the walls.' Most of my teaching energy ever since
that meeting has been towards encouraging the greed – not only to
read what's on the walls, but all sorts of other things; and, not only
to read, but also to write.

Even so, critical reading of the writing on walls is an important
part of literacy work. As a particularly good account of this reading,
which also addresses the relation between literacy in English and
other languages, I recommend a story by Marion Molteno.[1] In it, she
describes how the English teachers of Asian women learned to read
the racist graffiti on the walls in the streets with new eyes, and, over
a period of two years, developed a campaign to erase them. Early in
the story Jill, one of the teachers, tells of her conversation with the
husband of Siddiqa, the Bangladeshi woman she is teaching in her
home, about his reluctance to allow his wife to come to the class in
the centre, where she could meet other women. He tells Jill of the
difference between her experience as a white woman in the streets
and that of his wife. Jill, later, notices writing she had not noticed
before, and rethinks her assumptions:

> Walking back with Siddiqa on Tuesday, I kept seeing awful
> graffiti scrawled all over the place – 'PAKIS STINK' on the
> pillar box, 'GIVE ENGLAND BACK TO THE WHITES' on the

wall of the old factory past the traffic lights, 'KILL THE WOGS' in huge letters on the railway bridge, and National Front symbols on walls – I must have passed about five of them just in that one journey. *I kept thinking, thank goodness Siddiqa can't read English.* If I was Asian and I had to walk past that lot shouting hate at me every day, I think maybe I'd prefer to stay home [my italics].

The story tells of the slow and complex development of an alliance between teachers and their students to create a successful campaign to paint out the graffiti. It's a story about good reasons for not reading the writing on the wall; it's also a story about letters and meetings, doubts and anger, and about white people deciding to take responsibility for an offensive use of literacy by other white people. The conclusion describes the arrival at the project of a young Gujarati woman, the daughter-in-law of one of the students in the class. Before, she said, she had thought these classes were 'a bit of a waste of time' and the teachers 'a bit patronising'. Now, having heard about the anger the teachers were feeling about 'this graffiti business', she was offering herself as a volunteer, because, as she put it, 'If they're doing that kind of thing, I'd better go and see if I can help.'

This chapter, as I've said, deals with the principle of *equality* between reader and writer. The ordinary relationship between authors and their readers is unequal. The author of published words – whether in the medium of graffiti, books or packaging – has a concealed identity; and however uncertain and vulnerable the writer may actually have felt in the act of composition, once their writing is public, especially in the form of print, it acquires an appearance of authority. Student readers, if they have not understood or agreed with what they read of this writing, commonly feel that the fault is theirs, not the writer's. Adult literacy education, I argue, has to do with a principle that says: literacy development is only possible if students, when they are reading, acquire a greater sense of equality with other writers; and when they are writing, with other readers.

In chapter 5 I described examples in which students begin the process of becoming authors. This process, as with other authors, means a move from uncertainty to authority. This time, the authors who have that authority are no longer strangers: they are themselves and their peers. Each time they see this happen, they are able to shift a little more of the burden of responsibility on them, as readers, to make sense of another writer's text. The responsibility is a shared one.

In the first section of this chapter I compare different practices of reading aloud as a form of public performance, or test. Next, I relate this to the celebratory purpose of 'reading evenings' and the value of applause and audience for the student writer. Third, I discuss the achievements of community publishing in literacy work in persuading the writer to trust the reader. Finally, I discuss how a writer can gain some distance from her own work and choose to be either friend or censor to her own and other people's developing writing.

READING ALOUD

At academic conferences, it is not unusual for someone to 'read a paper'. For half an hour or more, one person has the attention of a whole group to a set of ideas they have organised in writing, which they read aloud. The speaker reads out her or his written paper to a group, without interruption. [2]

Now, for most women and men deciding to join a literacy class, the one thing they fear that they may be asked to do is a version of this. Literacy teachers like me have learned, from experience, to reassure our students: no one is obliged, we say, to read aloud. For many adult literacy students, reading aloud has direct associations with public humiliation. The text being read was not theirs; the performance of reading it out loud to other people was a test, done to order.

I have found two eloquent references to this experience. The first is in a piece by Doug Meller, originally published in a community publication by literacy students, and republished in an anthology of writing from groups round the country:

> I remember a day in school, probably the worst I had when I was in school, when our form teacher called me out to read out the English lesson. What I used to always do was learn a page. Oh, I was just cheating myself really, but I always used to learn a page. I knew this page without even looking at it really. I went to his desk and he says, 'Right, start reading.' But he opened the book and he said, 'Not that page'. Obviously he must have known. So I was stuck at a new page. I was

struggling through it and I got stuck at this word and he got really ratty about it. He said 'I told you that word not two minutes ago.' So I said, 'Well, I'm sorry sir, I've forgotten it.' He says, 'Well right, you go down to Miss Blackburn's class.'[3]

This memory is introduced by a statement that 'the fear of not being able to read and write stems from the age of, I would say seven or eight'. The recollection is about the terror of performance: 'performing' the page to order. (The terror had very real justification; later, he says, the teacher punished him for getting it wrong a second time and 'bloody leathered me'.)

The second account is not of standing by the teacher's desk, but of being one of a class taking turns to read aloud. In an article by a literacy educator, the recollection is given as a quotation from an adult student named as Helen:

We always read round the class taking turns. We read a paragraph each. I spent the whole lesson working out which paragraph was mine so I could practise before the teacher got to me. I hated it. I got so embarrassed in front of everyone I always went red, especially when I made a mistake.[4]

Like Doug Meller, Helen speaks of the ordeal of anticipation: waiting for the inevitable moment when she would be called upon to perform, and dreading the possibility that she would get it wrong.

When I first started working as an adult literacy organiser, my job meant a lot of interviewing and very little teaching. My 1974 work diary recorded fifteen appointments with new students a week. Each of these appointments lasted half an hour. In each, I believed I had two things to do: to encourage, and to assess. In order to do the second, I would commonly ask people to read something aloud to me, in order to gain some idea of what kind of reading they found difficult. From 1974, as I spent more of my time teaching and had initiated the first groups in the scheme, I renounced this habit. Gradually (I'm not sure when) I stopped asking new students to read aloud, and I avoided asking students to read aloud in the classroom; using the time, instead, to discuss with them their experience of reading, or inviting them to read something silently and then say what, if anything, they found difficult about it. By that stage I had heard so many of them speak of the kind of humiliation recalled by the writers above, that I had become determined to abandon a practice that could revive it for them.

In 1975 two collections of student writing were published: the first issue of *Write First Time,*[5] and a collection by students in Cambridge House Literacy Scheme, called *Father's Cap.*[6] Both these publications were tutor-edited. In both cases, the writers published had sent in writing and seen it come out as a printed product, but had not been part of the process in between. They had not met each other.

The first such meeting I witnessed came later, in 1976. It was at a weekend of literacy students and tutors, together, some of them published in *Write First Time*, meeting to exchange experience of writing and being published. I think that event was the first time I began to see the possibilities of reading aloud as something which did not have to be either a test or a humiliation (or something that students themselves sometimes felt they wanted to do to show their reading progress). Reading aloud, instead, could be a chosen means of sociable literacy; a celebration of authorship; a way of sharing writing.

Then, in 1978, as a result of work with Write First Time, I began to go to meetings of another organisation, called the Federation of Worker Writers and Community Publishers (FWWCP). I remember going to 'readings' run by one or other of the writers' workshops which were its first member groups. The FWWCP's own annual meetings consisted, from the first, of combining 'readings' with the formal business of its organisation. Very soon after it was established, these meetings grew to weekends, which by now have a national reputation. [7]

This section has been dealing with one small part of literacy activity: reading aloud. I have begun with it precisely because one version of it has such strong associations with inequality (the testing/punishing teacher and the terrified learner); and I return to it later. So far, I have used it to introduce a principle of equality which says: readers are writers, readers and writers are equal, writers have the right to read writing (their own or other people's) to others if they wish: they also have the right not to. Readers who write are entitled to meet other writers with both the respect and the scepticism of an equal. Reading aloud to others, instead of being a test or public humiliation, on this basis, becomes a choice.

In literacy practice using the principle of equality, the student has two choices – the choice between reading aloud or not and the choice between reading their own or someone else's writing.

APPLAUSE AND AUDIENCE

Some years ago, a colleague described a reading evening to me which had been a celebration of the authors' newly published book about childbirth.[8] The way in which 'reading aloud' was used here was certainly not like a lecture; but the position of the readers in this context was far closer to that of the author of an academic paper than to that of the performer of a classroom reading test.

> One evening in Hackney, East London, nearly three years ago, a hundred people came to a party. There were many kinds of food prepared, including West Indian, Turkish, and Cypriot dishes; there was drinking; there was dancing. There was an exhibition on the walls, and half way through the evening, there was a pause, to listen to some of the people there read aloud from a book. The readers were the authors; they read aloud from pages in the book which they had written. In short, it was a publishing party, of a very unusual kind. For not only were the authors presenting their written work aloud, giving voice to the printed word; they had also edited, designed and collaborated in publishing their own book. More than that, they had worked together in the conception and drafting of other people's writing as well as their own. The making of the book had engaged all of them in a process of dialogue with each other. The product was not only the book, printed and silent, but the reading from it, and the response to it.[9]

Not many of us find performing our own work in public that easy; nor did all the writers who read, that evening. But a number of things certainly helped it feel more like a pleasure than a pain: not least of which was the sense of being in the company of equals. The significance of this kind of event can only be fully understood in the contrast it makes to that other kind of text-reading, with the teacher as judge and jury, and the other listeners as passive spectators. That evening in Hackney, by contrast, the listeners were collaborators; the readers were also the writers, and their audience, co-authors.

In June 1990, I spent an evening with some sixty adult literacy students at the Lee Centre, for an event designed to celebrate local literacy work in the context of International Literacy Year. The planning group of six literacy educators, between us, taught some fifteen different groups in centres around the Borough of Lewisham. We undertook to encourage our students, in twos and threes, to come to the event both to meet others and, in exchanging something of each others' literacy achievements, to celebrate their own. At an early planning meeting, enthused with ideas of celebration, I suggested we should call the event a 'reading evening'. Two people in the group were cautious; they argued, convincingly, that a number of their students would be put off by this and would find reasons not to come. 'Reading evening', we agreed, would suggest compulsory reading aloud – in this case, to a group of people largely unknown to the reader.

So we planned an event which offered the students a choice of three ways to share their writing. They were invited to come to the evening prepared to read something, but they didn't have to. They could choose, instead, to send in their writing a couple of weeks beforehand. (Two of the planning group took on the job of typing out these writings, and photocopying, enlarging and posting them up on the walls a week before the evening, so that both the people in the Centre and the participants during the evening could read and enjoy them.) Or, second, they could bring a piece of writing with them to offer for a magazine of the event – along with the writings sent in earlier. (Another member of the group later undertook to collect, type and print copies of this. On the evening itself we asked people to write their own addresses on large envelopes and contribute 50p to the cost, and the 'publisher' later mailed them with the final copy.)[10]

Actually reading their writing aloud on the evening itself, therefore, was only one option students could choose, out of three. Once people had arrived, were drinking, eating and meeting each other, we had to decide how this 'reading' would happen. First we agreed that this was to be more than a men's event. We agreed to make a positive effort to seek out and if necessary arrange transport for women students. There would be a crèche (which, predictably, was used by several women for their children, but no men). From experience of literacy student meetings and events with the Write First Time project[11] and at the Lee Centre over the years, it also felt important, once women had been persuaded to come, to ensure that they were equally represented in whatever readings did take place.

So in order to ensure equal representation of women and men readers, we drew up two lists on the board with ten spaces on each for names of people offering to read: one for women, one for men.

During the evening, members of the planning group went round the room asking who would be willing to read, and, gradually, names appeared on the list. The men's list grew to six names before we had any women offering. Seeing this on a list, with the planning group going round pointing it out, women students, reluctantly, agreed to meet the challenge and allow their names to go up too.

Then we began the readings – alternating between women and men. After each reading, I invited listeners to applaud, and then offer any comment that occurred to them to the writer. Mostly these were gentle appreciations. Sometimes the subject of the writing led to discussion of the issue, rather than of the writing (as did one on the poll tax). Always, the effort was to ensure that every writer received one affirmative comment about the writing itself.

After a first group of ten people (five women, five men) had each read, we had an interval. Several, who at first held back and said they didn't want to read their pieces aloud, now asked if they could be added to the list. Having listened to some of the other writers reading, and having joined in the applause for them, they felt encouraged to take the risk of doing the same. Many people who came to that evening spoke, as they left and in later weeks back in their literacy groups, of the 'friendly atmosphere' of the event: it was an atmosphere of equality.

TRUSTING THE READER

There was a period, in the late 1970s and early 1980s, when every literacy scheme in the country seemed to be publishing student writing and holding reading evenings. Ten years later, as one adult educator has put it, there seemed to be a 'sustained attack' on the 'participative humanist model of literacy work' (which she saw paralleling 'the attack on liberal education and the centralisation of the curriculum').[12] The last national list of all titles in print from adult literacy projects which was published in 1982 listed 120 titles.[13] Publications of the national Adult Literacy and Basic Skills Unit regularly stress the importance given at national policy level to student writing.[14] But no national list of student publications has appeared since 1982; and Write First Time, the national organisation promoting and publishing writing on a regular basis from 1975 was closed down in 1985. Grant officers have even been heard calling student writing weekends 'old hat',[15] and overworked and underfunded local literacy workers have less and less time for the work it takes to inspire and co-ordinate the idea of students working to edit and publish their own writing.

Publishing, as I have suggested, means making public. The process of choosing to move from private thoughts and feelings to public, written expression of them goes on every time a literacy group meets. A woman called Martina, in a publication created out of a residential writing weekend, illustrates for us how the social arrangements of an event dedicated to inspiring and experimenting with writing can decide someone to tell her own story. Listening to others led her to recall her own experience:

> Well, I was sitting here this morning talking or should I say listening to the girls and the lads talking about their experiences in their lives. I was very interested in what they all had to say. One of the subjects that came up was broken marriages. It was great to see how well they were able to talk about it. They were saying how the children love the ground their dads walk on when they come to see them and how they feel a bit sad about it as they (the mothers that is) have given their lives to the children and they drop them when he comes in. I myself am from a broken home.[16]

It is no coincidence that the rhythm and clarity of the writing reads as if Martina is speaking to us. She *was* speaking, during the weekend, before or during the act of actually composing the written text. The result on the page is bound still to hold something of the sound of a voice, as well as the look of printed symbols. She is writing, not only on her title, 'Growing up in a broken home', but on the subject of writing itself. Her story, and the inspiration to tell it, came from being a listener to the stories of the others.

This particular method of generating writing in literacy work encourages above all not only a skill in presenting (either in writing or speech) but a particular kind of listening. It is listening which makes our ear sensitive to language, to narrative and structure, to argument and sub-argument; but it is also listening which allows us to check those who listen to us, and ensure that we feel prepared to take the risk of letting them hear what we have to say. This introduction to a magazine of writing from a four-day course for women 'fresh start' students says something about the value, to writers, of this mutual attention:

110

> We came here to learn and share experiences. In this magazine, we are trying to show some of the ways in which we learned.
>
> The women who came were from different backgrounds and cultures; of different ages and colour . . . . We hope these writings will evoke memories for us, and give others a glimpse into the lives of the twenty-four women who came together on this course.
>
> We began as strangers to each other. As we talked and listened in our groups – in rooms, dining hall, on a boat, on the lawn – trust grew, and so did we.[17]

It is oral work of this kind which gives buoyancy and flow of a particular kind to the finished written work: the springy step of a writer trusting her reader.

There's a similar feeling, of course, to those academic conference reports which publish, not the written paper presented or sent in later, but the verbatim transcripts of their author speaking at the event. This extract from the published report of a conference I attended, for example, takes me straight back to the hall of some three hundred people where I listened to the voice of the speaker: and for readers who were not there, the particular style of the written language offers an immediate sense of that audience, and her sense of their attention:

> It is inspiring to take part in these discussions. I can remember the days when literacy was regarded as just a matter for schoolmasters and technocrats; I can remember the time when literacy and liberation began to be talked about, but as a slogan for people in libraries and not really in relation to people whose lives it affected. I'm therefore very encouraged by the theme of this conference, the attitude of the people who organized it, and the numbers of you who are here today.[18]

This is a writer that I *heard*, at the event; only now that her text is printed do I, and others, see it, on the page.

As Michael Clanchy has pointed out in his study of medieval literacy, reading was once an entirely auditory exercise. The listeners heard a reader read the text; sometimes they heard the author himself read his own text to them, sometimes not. In our modern sense of the term literacy, the literate of that period were a tiny élite. Yet reading, then, would seem to be more equally available than now. It was available to all who could hear:

> 'Reading aloud and dictating permit the non-literate to participate in the use of documents . . . whereas reading and writing silently exclude the illiterate. When the voice is used, the clerk or scribe becomes no more than a medium between the speaker or hearer and the document. Neither the hearer of the book nor the *dictator* of a letter needs to be a master of every detail of the scribal technique himself, just as modern managers are not required to type or to programme computers.[19]

The most familiar modern equivalent to readers listening to a reading is television viewers listening to a newsreader. She or he, as 'clerk or scribe', sits in the studio and reads to us (from an autocue, rather than a parchment). We listen to (and watch) them reading: we read them, as they read to us. There is, of course, a deliberate illusion created in television newsreading: namely, that the newsreader is not reading anything at all, but speaking directly to us. In addition, unlike a gathering in a square, church or royal court, the newsreader cannot see us; and for our part, as television viewers, we are not usually aware of being in company with a throng of others (the other several million 'readers' being scattered across the country, or globe). This 'mass communication' system is paradoxically as private a literacy experience as silent book reading. However, news programmes sometimes mean watching something more akin to the medieval literacy practice. Film clips of politicians addressing a press conference or party congress show them reading, from behind a lectern or on a podium, from a sheaf of papers to an assembly of listeners. (In front of them, we also glimpse a very twentieth-century bouquet of microphones, a barrage of cameras – and a cluster of reporters, taking notes). [20]

Watching the television news is about as far removed as possible from listening to an author giving a 'reading' to a group. In the first case, nine million people scattered in different rooms across the country watch a person who cannot see them read a text that they pretend is not there. They do not tell us who wrote the text. In the second, a small number of people in the same room listen to a person they can see (and may already know, as a fellow student) reading something they have already declared is their own writing. The writer is reader, too. In taking this position, as I have suggested, she is deciding to risk trusting her readers. They, in turn, hear the writing and see her.

FRIEND OR CENSOR?

In chapter 5 I described some of the processes entailed in moving writing from private to public. In the last section of this chapter, I want to relate one of these processes to the principle of equality: namely, the process of editing.

Asked the question 'What does an editor do?', many people's first answer is: 'Cut'. (Almost exactly parallel to this view of editors, in my experience, is a popular understanding of the role of chair of a meeting. 'What does a chair do?' 'Stop people talking too much.' In chapter 7, I discuss some ways to explore a more optimistic view of both chairs and meetings.) This view sees the editor as the person who says you have written too much.

Good editors, like good gardeners, do sometimes cut, or suggest places where the text could be pruned; but only in order to introduce more light and ensure good growth. They see the work of editing not as arbitrary deforestation, but as fertilising, sowing, weeding and cultivating. The first thing any editor does, however, is to read the writing; and the first rule of editing is that it is always easier to be an encouraging, rather than censoring, editor to someone else's writing in process than to your own.[21] My experience as teacher-researcher has shown me, time and time again, that this rule applies to all inexperienced writers, from students in literacy classes to undergraduates on study skills courses. For this reason, in teaching editing skills, I have found it useful to be a teacher-instructor, and offer students three other rules in editing their own writing:

1 Leave time between being the writer and being the reader. Let the writing cool down, if possible for at least ten minutes. If it's a longer piece, allow an hour – or better still, twelve hours – between putting down your pen and picking up what you have written to read it through.

2 Treat the writer (that's you, in this case) as a friend. The advice you will offer should be intended, not to depress, but to help this friend.

3 Remember the effort of the writer. Your job is not to jump in and pick the work to bits. Read the piece as a whole. Decide what you

think is interesting or what you like about it, first, and say so. Only then offer suggestions as to what could be improved.

Bearing in mind the first rule, the best way to encourage students to develop – constructively edit – their own writing is to give them experience of editing other people's. Teachers have immense experience of doing this: which may explain why so many teachers write books. Week after week, we read and give feedback on essays, stories, poems, autobiographical pieces by people we know as our students. It sometimes feels like a chore; it is also, for our own writing development, a privilege. We have had the chance to think about what makes us want to read the text in front of us; what makes the writing interesting to us, as readers; what disappoints us; what inspires us; and what we find it useful to suggest to writers that they leave out, add or rewrite. Our job in trying to apply a principle that says 'readers are equal to writers', is to offer our students some of that experience.

Our culture of silent print does not make this easy. Much published writing seems to have said it so much better and so much more authoritatively than feels possible to the writer inside us. Writers in print are strangers to us. Teaching writing, then, means persuading the student writer that the writer they are reading is also human; also had to sit down and persuade themselves to put one word in front of another; and also only found out what they were going to say by actually saying it. It is hard to believe this when the published document has no author's name to it (as is the case in quantities of advice, policy or planning documents) – and all the more important to demystify some of the processes that went into such writing. [22]

In a classroom setting, the conditions are ideal for a reversal of some of this sense of inequality. All that is needed is to offer the invitation to students, at a certain stage in their work, to act as each other's editors. My approach is to offer it as an exercise. Each student gives a piece of the writing they are working on to another. Before they read it, I ask the group to apply rules (2) and (3) above, and to read through with me the following checklist:

1 Has the writer told you all you need to know?
   (Does it make sense? Is there anywhere where an extra word or phrase would make the meaning clearer?)
2 Has the writer told you all you want to know?

(there may be bits which interest you, and you'd like to know more.)

3 Is the writing in the right order? (maybe there is a bit nearer the end which would fit nearer the beginning – or the other way round.)

4 Does it begin and end well? (Do you want to go on reading after the first two sentences? Does the ending satisfy you?)

5 Has the writer said something too many times? (Sometimes we repeat a point in writing because we are not sure that we have said it clearly already. As the reader, you can help the writer to cut repetition; if the same thing is said twice or three times without adding anything, the writer may be losing your interest).

6 Has the writer written in a style that is comfortable to her or him? (We sometimes write in 'borrowed language'; because we feel our own way of writing is 'not correct'. This is a hard one for us, as readers, to assess. It sometimes helps to ask ourselves: are there words she/he could have used that would have been more personal or more expressive?)

7 Is there any 'proof-reading' that needs doing?
(offer a pencil mark on any words which look misspelt, or any places in the text where, as reader, you feel you could do with punctuation to be clear about what the writer means. The writer, later, can look again at the bits you have marked, and decide if she or he agrees that corrections are needed here.)

Gatehouse Project in Manchester, since 1977, has developed unique experience of editorial work with literacy students, bringing their writing to publication. This work usually involves three stages. First, to work with the writer, clarifying and organising the writing. The second is to pilot the finished draft with an editorial group or groups – consisting of literacy students and tutors – together with the writer. The third is to complete the writing, with developments and additions, and prepare it for publication. Stella Fitzpatrick, commenting on the second stage, points out:

> We all approach the idea of commenting on someone else's writing cautiously. Adult Basic Education groups are particularly wary and often cannot be selective at first. They value all writing because they know how hard it is to write and so initially it can be enough to read through with the aim of absorbing the message.[23]

115

In my experience, it is precisely this caution and care for colleagues' writing that student writers need to give in turn to themselves. The attention to ensuring that criticism is constructive, not negative, needs to be given equally to the reading of another writer's work as to the rereading of their own. John Glynn, speaking at a time when he was working with Gatehouse, told of his personal experience, as a previous literacy student, of the importance of this care and attention to others' writing. He was also clear, however, about the value of offering constructive comments to other writers – and about how this dialogue with others had, in turn, suggested a connection he could make with his own writing:

> Somebody would write something, and I'd see that, and to me, that could be done better. I felt I was going back to people and saying, 'Look, you can do better than that, I know you can, you probably don't' – and I probably hadn't made the connection with myself. You can see it on other people[24]

The interview from which this is extracted gives an interesting indication that his work as a Gatehouse editor in collaborating on the development of others' writing for publication had not only led John to reflect differently on his own writing, but also to extend his repertoire of writing purposes.

Stella Fitzpatrick reports on two editorial processes in Gatehouse's work: one, with a publication by five authors; the second, with one by a single author, Carol Millbank. The editorial group for Carol's book, she tells us, consisted of twelve people, of whom seven, like Carol, were disabled. Prior to their meeting they received copies of the draft of Carol's book, which they read in the classes or groups they already attended. The discussion of their comments for Carol at the meeting was taped: and the tape and notes were then the basis for Carol's further work on the writing with Stella. This example of the comments offered to Carol from one of the editorial group is, in my view, a fine example of a question made on equal terms from reader to writer: 'You mention names a lot. As a reader I take in so many names and then I get frustrated. Are you mentioning names because people might get hurt if you don't?'[25] Stella describes the meeting of readers/editors as 'simmering with activity' and concludes that in this process, all three parties concerned stood to learn: the writer, the editorial group, and the editor/publisher. The report as a whole is a remarkable testimony to the honesty and self-criticism of the latter.

Course groups with an interest in producing publications of their own writing have particularly good reason to address the issue of editing. This time, the questions which apply to a single piece of writing have to be extended to relate to a collection, with a self-consciousness about a wider readership. In chapter 5 I described an approach to 'making a book' used with one course. Another (the 1981/82 Lee Centre 'New Horizons' course group) used the more usual idea of a magazine. After looking first at a range of commercial magazines, we began the project by discussing three main questions, which I offered in these terms:

1 What shall we put in it? (short stories, interviews, poems, reviews, letters, news reports, adverts, editorial comment, 'human interest' stories.)
2 What must we decide? (number of pages; the writings we want to put in and their titles; how to make them fit the space; the order in which we want them; what illustrations we want (if any) and where to put them; what we want to write as an introduction for the reader; cover design and title; print run – how many copies? publication date and reading date – shall we read it just to ourselves, or with other people, too?)
3 How shall we make decisions about the writing?
(a) Some things will be written, or started, already. Each writer will need at least one other reader, who can offer comments on the draft and suggest any changes to make it clearer; 'proof-read' the writing for any errors of spelling or punctuation, before it is typed. (b) Anyone who has no writing ready yet, or who wants to have a go at some, can work together with one or two other people on one of the areas that need covering – once we've agreed as a whole group on subjects that we want written about.

The resulting publication, 'Horizon Views', had a print run of 100 copies and included writing (by seventeen students) in all the categories suggested under the first question. The offer of these categories grew out of a course syllabus which had been providing an informal approach to literature and social studies. Writing their own poetry, short stories, book reviews and 'points of view' was already relatively familiar; students who had been so far slow in putting pen to paper gained new energy from the project to write one of these, or try their hand at news or advertisement writing. Between March and June, the weekly course meetings included exchanges of drafts and editorial comments in the group. As writers, they were moving from first draft to final product, with a process in which they could have some sense of equality with their readers, and gain new understanding of the work behind other published writing.

This chapter has discussed the point at which writing develops with an approach which encourages students to reveal their work to each other, and to gain a sense of recognition and inspiration. These, as Patricia Duffin said, have been the purposes of over thirteen years of student publishing by the Gatehouse project: 'We wanted to publish work that gives a sense of belonging and identity to other ABE students, that makes good reading, and that acts as a springboard for students' own writing.'[26] In the next chapter, I discuss how a sense of community, such as this activity may promote through publishing, may also be explored in what is usually known as vocational education.

7

VOCATIONS AND VOCATIONALISM

I have discussed the principles of *context, inquiry, authorship* and *equality* as if they are separate; but I have also tried to show how at any given stage of education with adults, all of them come into play. Equality is important before student and teacher ever meet, as well as during the activity of a course group. The principle of inquiry is one by which teacher and students are all engaged in a research approach. The context of each and every participant meshes with that of the course itself (is it in a further education college? a women's centre? a workplace training room?). The identity of the author is, I have suggested, as important as the text of what they have to say – whether this is in the medium of film, publicity leaflet, poem or formal letter.

In this chapter I want to consider the principle of literacy education as a catalyst for a sense of *community*. This may appear to be the most obviously all-pervasive of the principles I have been discussing. Like peace, a sense of community is something most readers would support. However, on the one hand there are myths about a golden age in the past, long gone, when we all felt part of 'a community'; and on the other hand, much is at work in our present culture which is advocating individual goals at all costs. For this reason, I have deliberately focused this chapter on the community principle in its relation to education promoted as 'vocational'. I wanted to suggest some alternatives to a perception of this education only in individualistic terms.

First, I discuss what a 'workplace as a community' might feel like, and suggest how an organisation's signs and messages may express how much it feels like one. Second, I relate ideas of 'convergence' and 'overlapping communities' to question the myth of the static community ('maps and communities'). In 'status and literacy', I compare the different status given to different uses of literacy by different categories of workers and suggest that, though starting from very different positions, both 'high-status' and 'low-status' workers face similar uncertainties in certain uses of literacy. Finally, under the heading 'communication and community' I describe two literacy situations (the phone message and the meeting) and how they relate to the an idea about 'community'.

THE WORKPLACE AS COMMUNITY

A community is not born, it is made. In that sense, workplace communities are no different from any other. Most of us can think of organisations where staff complain of not being consulted, recognised or listened to; where mistakes, delays and bad temper prevail, and where prejudice, discrimination and downright oppression permeate the whole fabric of the place. On a good day, a workplace that is a community is different. People greet each other by name, ask after each other's concerns, carry out tasks energetically, get things done on time, and everyone feels well treated – whether they be elderly or young, disabled or able-bodied, black or white, speaking English as a first, second or third language, female or male. Different interests and common concerns live together. People speak of there being good communication.

Uses of literacy abound in all sorts of communities throughout our lives: home, school, street, shops, religious organisations and clubs.[1] Calling any one of these a 'community', however, can often feel like wishful thinking. Thinking of 'work' as a place you go to ('I'm just off to work') may not conjure up for many of us a place of communality. At best, it's somewhere you get paid to be. Go into any workplace now, in the early 1990s, and even that seems a rare luxury, with talk of redundancies in the recent past or imminent future. What chance of any spare time for 'education' about uses of literacy for any common interests?

Ideas about adult learning which relate to 'community education' focused in the last two decades almost entirely on education with people who were already in, or could become members of, 'community groups'; people living locally to the community education centre. Ideas of adult learning which concern employment, on the other hand, have been commonly grouped under the heading of 'training', provided for people who work, or would like to work, in the same kind of employment or for the same employer. The word 'community' has not tended to be associated with this activity. Attempts in recent years to regard education and training as an integrated whole, and bring the two sets of ideas closer together, have been overtaken by government policies favouring 'vocational' over 'non-vocational' purposes for adult education and training.[2]

Fortunately, adult learning is too elastic to be so divided. Put a room of educators and trainers together and stories abound of those enrolling in courses apparently designated for 'leisure purposes' who also have jobs in mind; and others on in-service training courses aiming to improve their skills, who fully appreciate the value of 'getting together' with others in the same business and of discovering new ideas which may have nothing to do with the jobs they do. Both adult education and employment training contain elements of each other. Even the distinction between certificated and uncertificated courses will not stick when, on the one hand, students speak of joining certificated courses simply in order to 'stretch their minds', and on the other, students find courses funded as 'liberal' education are useful to better their particular job skills. To those courses which are defined as 'vocational' (and a growing number of previously 'liberal' courses may only find support of they are so designated), the principle of community offers a basis for recognising this elasticity, and giving a more generous interpretation to the idea of having a 'vocation' than simply the next rung up the employment ladder.

For a long time, literacy work in the UK touched on paid work only to the extent that students asked for help with filling in forms to get jobs. The pioneering NUPE Basic Skills Project in 1978 was the first effort in this country to address the literacy interests of people actually inside the place where they had paid employment.[3] The interest of this and other schemes of in-service training for manual staff lies in the attention they gave to the workplace, not merely as a series of ladders to be climbed, but as a place of communication. The principle of a 'community' that I am arguing for takes this one stage further. It suggests that people's uses of literacy in workplaces, as in other places, can be seen as more than a means to pursue individual career paths in a competitive context. They concern, as well, an understanding of 'work' as a place of common as well as individual interests, within which they and other workers exchange varieties of communication. This in turn implies an idea of some change to the usual balance of power: namely, from a position in which some people communicate and the rest have to read or listen to what they say, to one in which all may have reason to make communication, as well as receive it – writing and speaking, as well as reading and listening.

Community education commonly advertises its wares in all kinds of places where people work, with the intention of reaching 'the public'. We put up posters and leave leaflets in shops, dentists' waiting rooms, job centres, libraries, laundrettes, day nurseries, and so on, thinking about people from the 'local community' who come in and use these places as consumers. So it came as a surprise to me in 1981 when Iris, a prospective student for the 'New Horizons' course we ran at the Lee Centre, told me that she had learned about the course from a poster at work. Iris worked as a cleaner at the local health centre. Our poster on the walls, addressed (as we had thought) to women who came in to the clinics at the centre, had attracted her too. The health centre was her workplace; she had seen our poster when she was at work.

As a result of taking part in the course, Iris joined the student committee for the centre (known as the Planning Committee), and contributed to meetings discussing and planning the centre's programme of community education. She also left her job as a cleaner and enrolled on a one-year training course then sponsored by the Greater London Council in 'Land use and construction' which she thoroughly enjoyed. One of these outcomes could be described as 'personal development', the other, 'vocational'. 'New Horizons' was not a certificated course (although it later acquired accreditation under the Open College Federation scheme). It offered no promises of employment qualifications, but was a means for women like Iris, determined to find change in her life, to make that change happen.

Two years later (as I described in chapter 4), I set about doing some systematic literacy outreach for a course for employees in their workplace: in the college where I worked (and still do work), with a group of cleaners and porters. Encouraged by the example of the 150 Hours Scheme in Italy, and the NUPE Basic Skills Project in this country, I was investigating the possibility of a literacy course for people at work, in work time.[4] Of the people who came to that course, I have little knowledge as to any subsequent changes they made. Seven years have passed since the course, some of the staff who took part in it have left the College, and one has died. One woman told me, some months after the course, that it was the ideas and encouragement she gained from it that led her to enrol for a local 'Fresh start' course, and then a GCSE English class. She also left her job as a cleaner and got a job as a dinner lady in a school; but I think this change was more to do with a preference for the different working hours than anything that happened in the course. Two others I know continue to write – but not for work. For me, the importance of that course continued in a different way; I had (briefly) got to know the names and interests of other people who work in the same place that I do. To this day, we greet each other in the corridors, by name. In a workplace filled with strangers coming and going, these greetings remind me that this, and other communities, coexist within it too.

The idea of the workplace as a community, like the idea of a residential area as a community, depends on some knowledge of its geography. By this I mean both the physical layout of a place and the relationships between different parts of the whole. It's hard to feel we 'belong' to a place if we don't know how to get round it, let alone give anyone else directions. Signs and posters – the usual bread and butter of literacy classes focusing on 'social sight' reading – are only one way in which an organisation gives clues to this geography.

In this course (as I also mentioned in chapter 4) I used a diagram of the buildings, and asked the group to read it with me. We discussed points of the compass, and how we know which way the building lies. I then invited them, in pairs, to interview each other with five questions:

How long have you worked here?
When you first started work here, what impression did the building have on you?
Which bits of the place do you know best?
Which room do you like best?
Who do you know uses that room at other times?

The discussion that followed focused particularly on the impression of the place, and of the other people who worked there. This developed into an intriguing debate about status, clothes and language, led by the comment made by one woman, brought up in the Caribbean, who said: 'Back home, you know them by their dress. Here, when they speak, you know by their voice, not so much by what they wear.'

The principle of a community purpose for literacy development suggests a use for this kind of course beyond any benefits it may have for the students themselves, and different from any benefits that may accrue to the employer, such as 'increased productivity'. Sharing knowledge about different parts of the organisation, and perceptions of other staff who work there, offers the opportunity for ideas to be suggested as to improvements in communication of all sorts. Seen as a group working on the principle of research, students such as these have the capacity to inform others in the organisation, not only of gaps in communication, but also of ways to remedy and improve them.

The same group, in the same session, did a second exercise, following the study of the building diagram. On the table I spread out some two dozen photographs I had taken of signs and notices in the building. I showed them a sheet with boxes for four categories of notices,[5] with examples in each: warning ('beware of the dog'); command ('keep off the grass'); information ('ladies'); and invitation ('please come in').

We sorted the pictures and talked about them. A couple of students needed help in reading the more complicated signs. Our work revealed that few of the notices around the building were invitations. We then talked about the informal notices – the graffiti. One woman described these as 'messages between people who never meet'. This led to a discussion about the unwritten messages: of dirty cups, beer cans, abandoned plates from the refectory and general debris. We then talked about the messages that the cleaners themselves might want to leave. What was the point? two of them said. There would only be some graffiti in reply. But a third, who had made her own sign, 'Could you please leave this toilet clean as you find it. The cleaner', said that for a week after she put it up things had improved. In itself, a small point; a minor example of the numerous exchanges on detail between peers. The exercise was more than a straight literacy one in reading signs; it was a discussion about the authors and intentions of those signs.

At the end of the course and the study, I argued (as a good workplace trainer should) that there were two sets of things to be gained from this and any subsequent courses:

1 Benefits for workers (opportunity to get to know each other better; an increased sense of recognition for themselves; greater confidence, skills and information).
2 Benefits for management. These I argued to be: better information as to both the skills of and pressures on manual workers; better understanding of the relationship between their work and

the life of the College; and better communication, on paper and face-to-face, between employees and employers.

One practical outcome of the course was in a sense nothing to do with literacy, but an important illustration of the education such a group could give others. As early morning shiftworkers, working in otherwise unoccupied buildings, they described a health and safety problem that had not until then occurred to me about the college where I also worked. Dark streets, empty buildings; women on their own. As one put it, referring to the house in the side street which the college owns: 'Well, number 6 was a very nice job, but it was a bit lonely, because I'm a coward. Every time I had to open the door and put the light on, I think there is someone there waiting for me.'

The report recommended, as a result of several discussions on this, that the college should organise women's self-defence courses. The result, some time later, were two courses organised by the personnel office for women staff throughout the college; stimulated, in part, by the newly appointed personnel officer's reading of this report. Since that time, the number of cleaning and portering staff has been reduced, and the traffic of people in the buildings and consequent workload on both these groups have increased. It will take a renewed commitment of resources to prioritise their opportunities for education and training over that of other staff.

MAPS AND COMMUNITIES

Two other points need to be made in relation to the community principle and adult learning. The first concerns the idea of *convergence*; and the second, that of *overlapping communities*. By convergence I mean this: that people in any given 'community' have converged, at a particular point in time. Despite all the evidence to the contrary, there is still a myth that community means permanence. This myth has led to ideas about a once-upon-a-time land, where everyone lived together and knew each other and had always lived in the same place. This land is contrasted with a brutal world of reality, in which nobody cares and nobody knows anyone else, and everyone comes from somewhere else in the first place. The fact is, that in most situations, everyone has come from somewhere other than you; even if it's a different house in the street. The myth is sad, because it often expresses an individual's sense of loss for some time in the past when they felt known and recognised; and

125

because it denies the possibility of difference being exciting. It is also dangerous, precisely because it is hostile to difference.

In many literacy courses that I have taught, particularly those in workplaces, I have found it useful to have maps of all sorts to refer to. These maps provide a way for people in the group to locate themselves, both now and in the past. We can then see the places from where we have all converged to be, for now, in this situation, in this room; and realise that people who live or work here *now* have not always done so.

If the group shares a common employer, the maps needed will be local: the map of the workplace may be a map of buildings scattered across a whole borough, or county, or a group of buildings on one site. If it is an adult or further education class of people who live 'locally', the maps needed will also be local; but to do justice to these personal histories, it's essential to have national and global ones, too. The discussion and written work in the college cleaners' group (as I suggested in chapter 4) is considerable: about child-hoods, and about journeys, migrations and holidays, too. Such discussion has little to do with training job skills in cleaning. It has everything to do with mutual interest and recognition: a sense of *converging* to here and now.

The idea of overlapping communities is this. Any one of us belongs to several different communities at any one time. At work, we are seen to belong to the work community. But since we bring the whole of ourselves to work, we are also bringing other communities there, too. This means that education which is limited merely to the technical job of using machines tends to spread, in spite of the wishes of any teacher-instructor who is around, to other dimensions; and that the outcomes of any 'training' may be several, not all of them concerned with our improved skill with that machine.

Two examples. First Anita, who, as well as being a cleaner, did voluntary work in a youth club. She was expected, from time to time, to write short reports on the work. The course helped her feel more confident in doing this. Second Wynne, who as well as being a cleaner, was a member of the local Pentecostal church. She had, for a long time, wanted to write a hymn herself. The course helped her feel more confident in doing this (and led to her then deciding she wanted to learn to read and write music, as she wanted to feel independent of another member of the congregation who trans-cribed her music for her). No educator or trainer can control the outcomes or effects of any vocational course. Its benefits may have less to do with a purpose relating to improved employability, and more to do with participation in other communities.

STATUS AND LITERACY

Meanwhile, training for employment, and in-service training for staff, often seem to mean training to fit a system. With more and more jobs being part-time and/or temporary, and services being bought and sold between departments of the same organisation, so more and more forms need filling in, and less and less communication in any other way is possible. Cleaners who came to the 'fresh start' courses needed no training from me on how to do their jobs more efficiently; although, with local authorities being compelled to produce competitive tenders for their services, courses in efficient use of machines and chemicals were already a growing feature of supervisor training. Increased productivity (cleaning more spaces in less time) has nothing obvious to gain from workers' increased literacy: except in one respect. Together with pressure to deliver faster, cheaper services, employers are also expected to have evidence or 'assurance' of the quality of that service. Quality assurance means record-keeping about more and more elements of a job. Staff who hitherto had to do their job and go home, now have to give written evidence that they have done it. Record-keeping means, as one local authority training officer said (speaking of refuse collectors), 'Now, they not only have to do things; they have to do things and record that they have done them'.

Vocational education, literacy at work, literacy for work: what does it all mean? How is literacy education to be both relevant to work contexts and employment aspirations and at the same time persuasive, to an employer, of its uses for the organisation? It all depends, of course, on what this education or training is called and who it is seen to be for. Courses for managers in information technology or conferences among professional bodies debating current policies are all part of an idea about 'investment'. Investing means dividends; high-status staff, participating in such training, accrue more status, both to themselves and to the organisation. The reason such training is never associated with the vocabulary of literacy education is because it is assumed that, here, we are speaking about people who already have a sophisticated grasp of reading and writing, thank you; and that literacy refers to other people who need some help in that direction.

The reason courses and conferences for professionals or management are, in fact, workplace literacy education is precisely because they too deal with the language and writing of communication within and between workplace communities. The single most important difference between such courses and conferences, and communication skills training for manual staff is the difference in the status of the people who take part in them.

In 1958 UNESCO adopted a definition of literacy, which prevailed in the 1960s and early 1970s, that defined a literate person as someone who could read and write a short, simple statement about themselves.[6] In 1990 I asked two different groups to try and carry out this exercise: one, a group of eleven manual workers on a one-day course in 'communication skills' in Lewisham; the other, a group of some fifteen academics in a workshop on a national residential conference of higher education in Sheffield.[7] In both cases I explained my interest in the exercise: that it originated with a definition of literacy, and that the idea of being able to write a short simple statement about oneself seemed to me to be less easy than it sounded. Both groups were meeting in a work context. However, the first was meeting with a purpose to 'improve' their literacy; the second, with a more detached and theoretical interest in literacy generally, which I was about to bring closer to their own experience. For both groups were asked to use their own writing as material for discussion.

In asking them to do the exercise (which, on both occasions, I tried to do myself), I was wanting to explore the complexity behind the surface blandness of the definition. Who of us can choose a short and simple thing to say about ourselves, and be willing to let anyone else see it?

With the first group, I also said that the purpose of the exercise was to get them warmed up for the day and break the ice about writing. (The day ran 9.30–4.30 and was later to include discussion and exercises about letters, reports and job interviews.) I told them they weren't being asked to show anyone what they had written – but simply to spend a few minutes, after writing, exchanging reactions to the task. When they'd written, I asked them to say what had gone through their heads as they set about writing. These were some of the things people said they had been thinking: 'What am I supposed to be writing?'

(There must be a trick here somewhere: a short simple statement? Why?); 'How shall I start? Having started, how shall I keep going?' *(I*

128

can say my name is Agnes White. But then what?); 'Why are the others still writing and I've stopped?' *(They must be more interesting people than me, as well as better spellers)*; 'What I've written about looks silly. My writing doesn't flow: it's just short statements.' *(You'll think I am stupid)*.

As I said, I had tried to clarify my reason for suggesting they do the writing. Even so, the first – double – question was one which many in the group said was dominant. (What does she want me to do? and – why is she asking me to do it?)

In the second group, the academics, I also explained the idea was for us to try out for ourselves what it felt like to write something 'short and simple' about ourselves. My hunch was that there would be literacy difficulties of a different kind. I also wanted to see how people felt, this time, about showing their personal writing to each other. This was a conference, after all, of people very experienced, in the workplace and in our daily lives, in writing for public reading. I wanted us to remember a bit of the exposure asked of literacy students when we invite them to pass their handwritten draft to someone else in the group; and to remind ourselves of the contrast between writing publicly and academically, and writing about ourselves, in the first person. So when this group had stopped writing, I asked them to exchange their card with their neighbour, read it, and offer them a response.

It's a common view that academics write academically – which is usually taken to mean verbosely. So it's easy for me to remember, from this group, the person who wrote more than was meant by 'simple'. And it would be easy to make from this a general case that academics are a lost cause when it comes to simplicity and personal writing. The individual concerned had written a multi-clause statement about his job and his interests; his partner suggested this didn't qualify as either short or simple. With his agreement the statement was read to the group; on the whole the group agreed – it was neither short nor simple. He disagreed. It was, oddly, an uncomfortable moment. The man was defensive, and plainly felt criticised. In a curious way, after all, he had just demonstrated that he was 'illiterate'.

Having said that, this was just one in the group; and the discussion we had was otherwise open-minded and stimulating. I invited this group, as I had invited the first one, to give their reactions to doing the task. People's thoughts had been, on the whole, exactly similar to what could be summarised as the three uncertainties raised by the first group: uncertain purpose – teacher's or mine? (what am I supposed to be . . . ?); uncertain content – how do I start? and keep going? and why is everyone else still at it?; uncertain form – it looks silly (so I'll look silly, too).

My own thoughts on the exercise are these: every statement any of us makes about ourselves is complex and context-bound; and both the form and the content are determined by the idea we have in our heads of the reader. All three uncertainties, indeed, add up to an uncertainty about readership: who is this for?

Is literacy training for work to be rehearsals of literacy events in employment? If so, this exercise, arguably, appears at first sight to have little to do with the working lives of either university lecturers or van drivers. The important thing about it, though, is that it invites people to think about the complex uses we all make of literacy, the choices that are open to us as to what we say and how we say it, and above all, the question of who we are imagining our reader or readers to be. It also brings us to the issue of different kinds of literacy having different kinds of status. Ken Levine[8] has made the interesting point that there is a distinction in status between the 'correct' literacy expected of non-status workers and the 'creative' literacy expected of those in positions which command 'high public esteem'. Possibly the 'illiteracy' of the individual in the second group with whom I tried out this exercise was the result of his assumption that he should be 'creative' rather than 'correct'. Low-status jobs ask for literacy that is low-status: reading labels, completing dockets. High-status ones expect expository prose.

COMMUNICATION AND COMMUNITY

There are a number of literacy events[9] commonly associated with getting and keeping a job. I want to pick out two: the phone message and the meeting. One way to teach strategies for all these and other 'vocational' moments is to offer ready-made scripts as exercises for the students. (In *Learning from experience* I offered two scripts, for example, of letter-writing situations, in which students were asked to take up the position of one or other participant in a story of an accident, writing formal letters seeking redress for some wrong they had experienced.) I would now call this approach the 'formula writing' approach. It has much to be said for it. Students enjoy it. They are given worksheets and questionnaires to answer and exercises with sample texts to work on.[10]

Sometimes, however, it's worth getting the group to use their own considerable experience to create the situations themselves. This is particularly useful when the group shares a common employer – even if they work in different buildings or departments, doing different jobs. As I have already suggested, they will know far more than the teacher could about the structure of the organisation and the norms and culture of its methods of communication. To invite a group to create their own 'script' from which they can then act out – in speech and writing – the appropriate roles releases a different kind of energy from the group than 'formula writing', and it often clarifies better the reality within which they actually have to perform these tasks in the workplace context.[11]

The phone message

This is a lot less easy for the teacher to control than a ready-made exercise, and can therefore be somewhat nerve-racking. Say there are ten people in the group. They are asked to divide up into two groups and think up a situation for a phone message. What happens next, depending on the group, may be quite a lull. Then, suddenly, one person tells a story of a phone message she has had to take; another caps it; they discover they both had to deal with the same hospital official ringing up; the conversation turns to other occasions (nothing to do with phone calls) when they have had to deal with this person. Someone remembers a friend who was a patient at the hospital and the trouble they had with their treatment. The room is buzzing. The teacher watches the group's faces, leaning towards each other and interrupting, talking across each other, capping one story with another, and the old fear of the literacy teacher – they're just talking: when are we going to get down to the real work? – surges up in her mind. Eventually, she calls 'Time's up' – and, to her surprise, both groups are ready with a phone message situation.

The day this happened to me, I was working, again, with a group of care assistants employed in residential homes for the elderly, on a half-day 'report-writing' course. Rather than taking this course title literally, I proposed the phone message exercise in response to the comment several of them had made at the outset that 'I can't write as fast as people talk'. This statement could have led – and in other groups has led – to the job of taking minutes in meetings, which we will come to in a moment. The purpose of the exercise, as I suggested it to them, was about practising taking down in writing, for someone else to read, a message given orally – in this case over the phone.

Group A was to provide the message, with one of them being the person on the phone making the call. I was given the part of the person taking down the message, asking questions and answering the call. Group B's job was to do their best to take notes from the conversation in order to record the message in the appropriate log book. While I was acting the part of the 'receptionist', I also undertook to try to take notes from the message myself on the flipchart (turned away from both groups). There were two message situations: (i) GP rings up hospital and speaks to bed allocation officer (me) – the GP is trying to establish if there is a bed for a patient at the residential home who is in a diabetic coma; and (ii) hospital nursing sister rings up residential home and speaks to care assistant (me) – she wants to report that the doctor has examined Mrs T, our resident (and currently their patient), and found that she has a fracture of the left femur; she wants the relative's phone number for a consent form.

In having to teach me their situations, the group was making conscious the working relationships within which their communication skills and literacy were being used. In both cases, we agreed that the person receiving the call was likely to be subject to interruptions, surrounding noise, and other things she was in the middle of. What we were trying to bring to life, then, was the reality of the literacy context. The job of actually writing down the essential information from the call was more than a worksheet exercise which could be carried out in the relative calm of the classroom: it was an exercise in concentration in the middle of confusion. My job, as teacher, was to offer techniques for personal shorthands, help out with spellings, and to remind people of their entitlement to stop the caller and check what they needed to know in order to get it down in a way they could turn into a message report as soon as they had a free moment. What I learned was that, for some in the group, the idea of shortening words was new, and what worried them was whether, later, they could turn a personal abbreviation into longhand. Methods for 'taking notes' proliferate in study skills courses for students in academic courses; this was a useful reminder to me that the confidence in your ability to convert the notes back into intelligible prose is no less a confidence to be practised and learned.

The anxiety about 'writing as fast as people talk'[12] at first may seem something to be resolved by teaching people to listen, stop a caller, and make time to write down the key words or phrases from the message. Actually, it can also be, as with this group, about learning to make up personal shorthands and to trust them. For me, and many other people used to writing a lot on a regular basis, the use of abbreviations (such as cttee, bldg, hosp., pple, dr, s'one) is, after years of taking notes in lectures and meetings, second nature. For groups such as this one, the confidence needed was a confidence in their capacity both to invent a code they could use for private notes and to be able to translate it into meaningful sentences for public writing.

This group, from their specific work experience, proposed phone message situations that were from one organisation to another (health service to social service) and which needed recording in a book. During another workplace course, this time attended entirely by male workers in the local council's environmental services, the messages proposed were all internal to the organisation: that is, from one council employee to another, of another rank, which in most cases required the more common situation of producing a written message to pass on to another individual. The examples this group offered, again from their own experience, were these: from roadsweeper to office, to ask why the two bins requested had not been delivered, and when they would be; from office to porter, to request he change his rest day to accommodate a change of party booking of a hall from a Saturday to a Friday; from porter to office, to ask for authorisation to give the go-ahead to a gas board worker to fix a gas leak; from roadsweeper to office, to request breakdown service for van broken down.

The person answering the phone is often, as receptionist, a messenger; it is not them, but someone else, for whom the message is intended. Frequently, then, there are three, not just two, parties involved in a message: the message giver, the messenger, and the message receiver, who is the person then expected to take action or make a decision. Breakdowns in communication can happen at two key points: between message giver and messenger and between messenger and message receiver (the messenger passing on at second-hand the information or request to the person it is intended for).

With this group, we carried out an exercise in which we tried to examine these two key moments, using the message situations they had generated. The fourteen students and two tutors divided into two groups. From each group, one person agreed to be the messenger.

133

These two people left the room. Choosing one of the message situations, the two groups then briefed another of their members to be the message giver. The group as a whole was then to act as the message receiver of the message they had themselves devised. Messengers came back into the room, and in two corners listened to the message from the message giver. They then rejoined their group and gave the message to the group as a whole. At the end of the exercise, the groups wrote down what they saw to be the message which the messenger needed to write down in order to make absolutely clear to the message receiver what it was. (As part of the exercise, I stressed the importance in any written message of including the usual key ingredients of time and date of call, name of caller, and name of person the message was addressed to.)

These and countless other exchanges of speech and writing are the everyday communications of an organisation, on which depend both its internal sense of community and its quality of service to the public. If we rank the four literacy activities of speaking, listening, reading and writing in order of priority, it's interesting to note that, in this exercise, reading comes bottom of a list headed, first and foremost, by the abilities to speak clearly and listen accurately, followed by some strategies for writing down the essentials.

The meeting

What is the point of meetings? And what is the purpose of having any written record of them? Before introducing the conventions of agendas, minutes and the meeting chair, I have found this a useful question to discuss in workplace courses. Weekly meetings of staff in any organisation are not always recorded in writing. The problem this raises can be a lack of accountability. Remembering what was decided, and who said they would do something about it, becomes an uncertain business. Several groups I have taught have had experiences of meetings that are either boring and frustrating, or both. Much of this boredom and frustration originates in a sense that 'it's pointless, we never get anything done'; 'there's all this talk, but nothing gets decided'. Meetings, good or bad, are a live expression of any organisation's sense of community. Their effectiveness depends on a clarity as to both the rights and the responsibilities of people involved. This means being clear as to who is chair, and why; what the agenda is, and who decided it; and which decisions are to be carried out by whom.

In any class, with this as with any other topic introduced, it's important to establish the group's experience. Meetings they have been to (at work, at their children's school, where they live), as well as meetings they have avoided going to. In an article addressed to a largely academic readership, I described what I then saw to be some of the problems and a possible solution, quoting from a woman's explanation to me as to why she had never felt able to join in with any campaign group:

> 'People like me, who aren't educated,' she said, 'we don't speak properly. So when I go to meetings, and I hear all these other people talking, I don't open my mouth, in case I get my words all mixed up. It's not that we don't care about cuts, it's just that we don't have the confidence.'
>
> Her problem, however, is not with her own language, but with other people's: the vocabulary she hears used by 'educated' people, in meetings or on the media. As a small solution on such occasions, reading aloud the minutes of the last meeting at the beginning of the next allows everyone in the room to share, as a group, in a continuity of work. It is an example of how we could all make a more conscious attack on a privatised idea of literacy, and I suggest it has two possible effects: it could collect the minds of the people there, and it could encourage the minutes secretary to write less.[13]

The 'minutes secretary' in my mind then was the kind of person who, like the man at the conference described earlier in this chapter, might have more difficulty in writing a short and simple statement than in writing a long and complex one. Others, contemplating the prospect of having to write a record of a meeting, have other difficulties with their literacy. Ken, in interview recorded some years ago, offers a good illustration:

> The tenants' association was missing a secretary. Tom never knew I couldn't read and write. Right? And he nominated me to be that secretary, and invited me to a meeting that night, not knowing exactly what I was walking into! See, and I sat at this table, and he turned round and he said to her – I was on the tenants' association, and I used to, like, the odd members, go out and pick up the pamphlets and deliver them, things like this: odd jobs that I didn't mind doing, because I knew there was a meaning behind them, see.

And, 'Well, that's settled then', she said, the woman there, the chairman. I said, 'what's that?' And she said, 'You're now secretary!' And not knowing exactly what that meant, I accepted. When they put that book in front of me, and all that paperwork, I was just about paralysed where I was sitting, see! I said, 'Er – oh, right'; but I didn't ignore it, I took it away with me, and I was kept looking at it indoors. And I was so hurt, that I couldn't do it. So hurt, that something I was so interested in, and I'm lost. I've got to hand it back.[14]

This may be a case of what Levine has called 'induced helplessness':[15] someone who has defined themselves as beyond help, and who cannot conceive of self-help. What is striking about the account, however, is Ken's enormous sense of disappointment felt at having to refuse being able to contribute to a community of which he already felt an active member. (At the time of interview Ken was meeting a literacy tutor regularly; and he later joined a group. This conversation was by way of being a recollection of times past.)

There are, as I have suggested, sentimental associations with the word 'community'; and it may seem naïve to suggest that workplaces could have anything to do with it. Workplaces are also sites of struggle. Workers, historically, have had to create their own communities of protection and campaign with the purpose of claiming and achieving basic conditions of employment. In the latter half of the twentieth century many people have had little reason to expect any sense of 'community' at work; and women, being the majority of part-time workers, especially so. Yet this principle remains an important one in addressing the genuine interests anyone in unskilled or semi-skilled jobs may have in literacy. If education and training opportunities are to have meaning, it is to their interests, rather than to other people's version of their 'needs' that such training should be addressed.

Daisy, a black woman who talked with me in Sheffield, worked nights as a care assistant in a residential home for the elderly. Strictly speaking, her job (then) made no particular literacy requirements of her. She spoke of the course she had attended in work time:[16]

There's people there what can't do anything at all, you see. But I am not that bad, thank god. I can read and write. It's just I spell the way I talk, you see. I drop my s's and r's or something like that.

Daisy's account to me of becoming a shop steward contains two attractive features. First, the pride with which she tells of her being good at – and respected for – her ability to speak up for herself and her colleagues. Second, the humour with which she refers to the sheer quantity of paperwork she had undertaken as a result of accepting their nomination:

So he says, 'Go on Daisy, be a shop steward, we haven't got one here' – because they know I can talk up for myself and they know I can talk, you know. I learned to survive – because you've got to learn to survive, and I learned the hard way.

I says, 'Well look, no-one is going to walk upon me; you can do so much, but then I'm going to say "Look, that's enough. Enough is enough".'

So they says, 'Go on, go on, represent us.'

I said, 'Alright then, I'll get a form.'

So I've written off to the union for a form, and they sent me a form, and a whole – well, I've cleared them out now, but a month ago, you couldn't see! In here was books and books and books. There was thousands and hundreds of books and papers – you know, that they sent me; because when you're a shop steward every morning three and four letters come through the door, telling you all things, about things. So they sent me this form and I filled it in. Never knew what I was going in for!

Representing others, a theme with which this book begins, is an important aspect of workplace democracy, and an important purpose of literacy. Daisy had learned 'the hard way' to speak up for herself; speaking up in meetings, on behalf of those who had elected her to represent them, grew from the strength she already had. The 'vocation' she was following was something she already knew about; the paperwork was the price she had to pay. The skills she needed in 'vocational' training were the skills to transfer the strength and pride she had in representing herself to a situation where she had to represent others. Some of that would mean learning how to make the paperwork herself: writing the minutes of the meeting, as well as participating in it.

As I suggested earlier, it is commonly assumed that the job of chairing a meeting means knowing how to shut people up: the chair as a police officer controlling the traffic of talk. A more hopeful view of the chair is as someone who knows how to encourage other people to speak up. If a meeting is to feel anything like a community of people, I have found this job description for a meeting chair to be a useful one.

The job of a chair is:

To check that people know each other's names.

To check that everyone can see, or has a copy of, the agenda for this meeting, and the minutes of the last one.

To check if anyone has anything they want to add to the agenda.

To agree a time that the meeting will end.

To try to keep the meeting on time, and move on discussion if things are getting stuck.

But also:

To notice if anyone is remaining silent, or may be wishing to speak but has not yet spoken, and encourage them to contribute to the discussion.

To find out from the meeting when people are ready to make a decision.

To ask for a proposal, if there is none, as to what the decision should be.

To check who will be responsible for carrying out the decision.

To make sure that the minutes secretary is clear as to what she or he needs to write down at any stage of the meeting.

This is a rather more complicated, but also more attractive, set of responsibilities for a meeting chair than that of the police officer of talk. Students with whom I have discussed it have expressed surprise at the idea it expresses of a chair who not only has to lead discussion, but can also ask for help in doing so. They have even gone away talking of putting themselves forward to take a turn in chairing the next meeting they have to go to.

The last item on the job description offers a place for the minutes secretary which, again, many people usually see as a role they would do anything to avoid. They disqualify themselves from being capable of taking minutes, in the belief that they, and they alone, would have to get the notes of the meeting written both accurately (as a complete record of everything that was said) and correctly (in the proper kind of standard English). Minutes secretaries, in reality, are entitled to help during a meeting. They have the right to ask, at any given moment: 'Can I just check what I have written down here, to see if the meeting agrees with my wording?' Or, 'I'm not sure if I know what you want me to write down about this item. Can you just recap, chair, on what has been decided?'

It comes as an extraordinary piece of news to many people to know that the word 'minutes' at the start of a meeting agenda indicates a moment when the whole meeting takes responsibility for checking the accuracy of the minutes of the previous one. If there are omissions or mistakes, it is the job of the group to check and amend them. This activity is there not in order to pass judgement on the minutes secretary's failures to do a perfect job, but precisely in order to recognise that the record of a collective group is a collective responsibility.

8

CONCLUSION

In the introduction I said that all writing is a journey, and that literacy education means a journey towards confident authorship. 'Journeys' suggest a kind of purposeful line, travelling towards known or unknown destinations. However, of the five principles I have discussed, that of authorship is, in my view, not so much a point of arrival as a centre. Authorship is not the end of the line: it is the middle of the web; a central principle which others overlap, and to which they all refer.

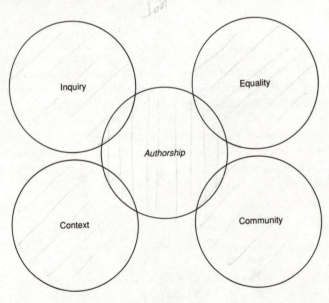

In the field of adult literacy education which I have been discussing, such a position depends on there being two others: first, an effort on the part of the educator to describe and promote the benefits and pleasures of this kind of learning, and second, an interest expressed by others in participating in that learning. The place where the expressed principles of literacy education and the expressed interests in such education meet and overlap is the place where issues of representation and truth collide. It is also the place where questions about educational practice, and about the principles on which it is based, are posed most acutely.

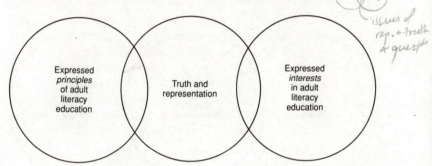

However, such bubbles move and, at times, float away from each other. At one time and place they are in one relationship to each other; at another place, and at another time, they are related in an altogether different way. The very ideas of context and inquiry imply that this must be so. Meanings and uses of literacy and equality shift with different social and historical contexts. And the two diagrams, in my account of things, must of necessity intersect with each other in more than one dimension. One representation of how this may be so could be in the shape of a third diagram:

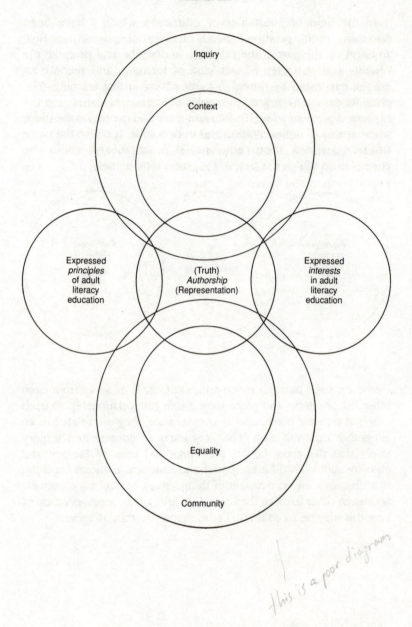

this is a poor diagram

CONCLUSION

This is an attempt to make interdependent a set of ideas which have been described as a chronology, one chapter (and principle) following another. Writing is linear, and, even with circles round it, one-dimensional. Life, on the other hand, is many different things at the same moment; and people relate to the same thing differently in different situations. It is always a risky business to attempt to parcel up into static categories the dynamic movement of relationships such as these, which fluctuate and shift in the process of adult literacy education. What I have attempted to do in this book is to sketch the issues and the set of principles which I have found to be important in my own learning as an educator in this process.

AFTERWORD

A book about literacy is, for its author, an education in literacy. Some of the advice I have learned to give my students about writing I always have to remember to give myself, as I travel through, round, up and down any writing. The old enemy, to which I referred in the Introduction, continues its work. (When I reread a draft chapter my first thought was too often: 'This is rubbish'. When I read something from another writer, too often, I thought: 'I could never write like this.') Yet again, I have had to learn to practise what I preach: to do what I recommended in chapter 6 on equality, that student writers should do: be good to yourself; recognise the effort; let it cool down.

In this Afterword I wanted to restate, in different terms, some of what I have already said about authorship and equality; and in particular, comment on the writer as reader.

Writing this has meant reading others' writing. After this section, as is the convention, come the Notes and the Bibliography: the journeys and the signposts. This is the first book I have written with a bibliography in this form. I had mixed feelings in the process of making it. If it had not been in the publishers' own guidelines for authors that I should list my reading in this way, I would have done what I have done in all previous writing: leave the references to the notes. But my reading of other books had depended on entering a reading community whose systems I had myself found useful. (I found Michael Clanchy's work, for instance, as a result of a bibliography from Brian Street).

Some books were accidental finds. It was a good friend who bought Marion Molteno's collection of stories as a present for me, little thinking how illuminating they would be for the bit of work I was doing at the time. I came upon Susan Hampshire's recent book when I was looking for something else, in a bookshop. I would not have thought of looking in Paul Fussell's study of the Great War for discussions of literacy use had Rodney Mace not pointed out a particular chapter to me, from his own reading. Still other books and articles (by Mary Hamilton, Bill Naughton, Sue Shrapnel Gardener) were old friends which the project of writing this book gave me reason to reread. New discoveries and new publications came into bookshops and libraries as I was writing. Other people's alphabetic lists, in these and other publications, led me to writers I would not otherwise have found; and in the week of drafting this Afterword, I am in the middle of reading four separate books, all of which I wish I had space to mix into this one.

Academic writing is a competitive game, and bibliographies have sometimes, when I've read other people's, looked like the author showing off: the longer the list, the more they've read; and most of the things they list I seem never to have heard of. They've read more than I have read. If that's how I felt, then I can't help wondering if that could be the effect that the Bibliography in this book might have on its readers.

Bibliographies, however, are more than a list of the writer's trophies or score-card in a literacy race. They are a celebration of other people's thinking; a recognition of them as sources of ideas and inspirations, of people with whom the author has tried to grapple; and, sometimes, a means of introducing readers to sources they want to pursue themselves. Nevertheless, such a list also appears as a catalogue of people, who, because published, have an aura of celebrity. It's a window display. This, too, has its flip side, to the person compiling it. The business of compiling a bibliography, like a lot of other literacy business, looks much less impressive when you do it yourself than when you look at it through the window. It is a list; or the sum of several lists, of the publications piled on the table and floor beside the word processor.

I made the decision to include some of my own writings among those which are given in this list (or score-card) because I deliberately set out in this book to argue with, comment on, and credit myself as a writer, along with others. In doing this, I feared the charge (from myself, if from no one else) of 'showing off'. One reason there are more entries under 'Mace' than for other names in the list is because I happen to have in my possession more of these short pieces than the countless short pieces also published by any one of the other names in the list. Another is that Mace (1979b) is the only book or writing of mine that I ever see in anyone else's bibliography; and I alone seemed to know that I had said other things since then in articles, rather than books. Mace (1979b) has been a burden to me: every time I have seen it referenced elsewhere I have silently cried out 'but I said it better later!' Mace (1979b) is in any case now out of print.

I have felt ashamed of Mace (1979b) and then, loyal in her defence. So, in the end, there has been a third reason that, above all, made me persist with referencing some of my own articles and publications among all the other reading: and that was, that I have been trying to write a book about contexts. I wanted to re-read, re-view, re-search, some of the thinking I had done myself, as well as that which others have done. I wanted to use principles of context and inquiry in re-examining both what I knew and what I did not know was also being said and written at the same time. Some of what I have written in the past has surprised and pleased me with its passion and interest. Other pieces and passages of mine I am ashamed to reread. They seem paltry, thin, insubstantial, partial. Yet I have read other authors, and come back to some of the things I have said, and managed to think: 'I said that, too.'

Both pride and shame are part of the writing feelings which our students deal with every day in their own writing development. The struggle to be honest about what it is we have changed *from* as well as what we want to change *to* is the everyday struggle of literacy education. Frank Smith says (or said: it was 1982 and he might himself say it differently now) that a writing teacher should never indulge in autobiography. Dirty word, autobiography. Not, I'm sure, in Frank Smith's thinking in general, but in the world of academic writing in general. What I've done in this book is begin some fragments of autobiography of my own. It is an indulgence. I don't apologise for it.

NOTES

INTRODUCTION

1 Reported in Mace (1983) and discussed in chapter 3 of the present study.
2 See Francis (1991).
3 The shortest and most accessible summary of the purposes of International Literacy Year that I have found is UNESCO (1990).
4 Hamilton (1987).
5 Reported in Mace and Moss (1988).
6 Charnley and Jones (1979).
7 Levine (1986).
8 M. Clanchy (1979), p. 7.
9 Mace (1979).
10 Mace (1980): the subtitle for this was 'Discussion and materials for adult groups studying the uses of language, literacy and communication'.
11 Mace and Yarnit (1987), Lawrence and Mace (1991).
12 Wendy Moss and I started the Diploma in Literacy and Adult Learning course at Goldsmiths' College, University of London in 1990. It is a two-year part-time course for staff with experience in adult basic education. Similar postgraduate opportunities have developed since the mid-1980s at the universities of Leicester, Lancaster, Sussex, Reading and Manchester. The Research and Practice in Adult Literacy (RaPAL) organisation grew out of a 1984 national conference at Lancaster University; see Hamilton and Barton (1985).
13 Smith (1982).
14 Kress (1982), p. 25.
15 Ivanic and Moss (1991).
16 The government white paper, DES (1991) explicitly ruled out central funding for 'courses catering for adults' leisure interests'.
17 Loewenstein (1983), p. 39.
18 Naughton (repr. 1974), pp. 112–19.
19 ibid.

147

CHAPTER 1

1 To an extent, this is a problem true of any adult educator describing any kind of adult learning: the first time it was made clear to me in this form was in a discussion about reporting on art education. In 1985, at the Lee Centre, two of us were trying to find a title for a series of five reports about community education that we were publishing. My colleague's report was an account, not of literacy, but of art and discussion work he had done with a group of homeless men. 'The problem I find in writing this stuff', he said, 'is how I can adequately represent the painting these men do: the process that comes about before the finished art work.' By restating his own problem, he solved ours: the title for the series, by mutual agreement, became 'Problems of representation'.
(Dave Rogers, 'Life chances', Lee Centre 1985. See archive sources listed at end of Bibliography.)

2 *Liberating literacy*, film and accompanying booklet, available on video from: Forum Television, 11 Regent Street, Bristol BS8 4HW.

3 ALBSU (1988), para. 16.

4 See Hughes and Kennedy (1985).

5 Mace (1979a).

6 *Birmingham Evening Mail* ('Priorities of people who can't read'), 18 September 1976.

7 Joseph Loo Bianco, foreword to Wickert (1989).

8 Street (1990), p. 10.

9 Brian Street (1984), p. 218 quotes Levine as suggesting, in a paper called 'Becoming literate: Final report on a research project, "Adult literacy and the socialisation of adult illiterates"' that Mace (1979b) sees adult illiterates as 'lacking in self esteem' and in need of 'comprehensive resocialisation' and that all I 'offered' was 'a project for altering the individual's consciousness' which will 'remain marginal if it fails to challenge central establishments themselves'. I was confused and a bit irritated when I first read this; I couldn't find where they had found this in my book, and thought I'd said other things than this. Later, I reread it, and understood their impression slightly better, although I still disagreed with it. I also remembered that all writers are open to multiple readings, and stopped minding.

10 One such account begins at a different time of day: 'It's raining; it's cold; it's June; and it's seven o'clock in the morning. Thirteen women, eleven of them cleaners, in an upstairs room in Lewisham are thinking of words they associate with sunshine.' See Mace and Wolfe (1988). See also Part II, chapter 3 of the present book for more on this particular course.

11 Charnley and Jones (1979), p. 26.

12 Ibid., p. 62.

13 The World University Service (WUS) has played an important part in this change. See, for example, Marilyn Thomson, *et al.* (eds) (1991) *Aid and Women's Non-formal Education*, London: WUS.

14 See, for example, Mace (1981), (1986) and (1988a).

15 Gerry (1983), p. 25.

16 Charnley and Jones, p. 25.
17 Baynham and Mace (1986).
18 Hautecoeur (1990).
19 Letter to *The Evening News*, 28 January 1975.
20 Letter to ILEA *Contact*, no. 23, January 1975.
21 'Right to Read', British Association of Settlements, 1975.
22 See Risman (1975).
23 Kedney (1976).
24 UNESCO, Declaration of Persepolis, 1975, reproduced in Hamadache and Martin (1986), pp. 128–31.
25 *Looking for words*, made by United Television Artists for the Adult Literacy and Basic Skills Unit, for International Literacy Year.
26 Bryan, *et al.* (1988), p. 43. See also ibid., pp. 38–50, 89–94.
27 Linda's letter appeared in *Write First Time*, vol. 1, no. 1, July 1975.
28 See Mace and Yarnit (1987), pp. 90–2.
29 Clarke (1989), p. 10.

CHAPTER 2

1 Clarke (1989), p. 11.
2 See for example Woodrow (1987) and Evans (1992).
3 Marilyn Waring (1987) refers to the 'conceptual incapacity of statisticians . . . to define housework. and to recognise what is and is not labour', which, she says,

> is, exacerbated both by the great volume of work that women do and the fact that they do many chores at the same time . . . In my research I have encountered the constant irony that some of the best sources for information about the work that women do is published by the international office of the International Labour Organisation (ILO). This same ILO is responsible for the definition that concludes that the vast bulk of the labour performed by women is not work. (p. 186)

4 Britton, J. (first edn 1970; repr. 1972).
5 Britton, J., 'Writing to learn and learning to write' (first pub. 1972), in Pradl (1982), p. 100, 101.
6 See Charnley and Jones (1979), pp. 87–101 and Mace (1979), pp. 65–8.
7 George Ewart Evans (1977) gives an illuminating insight into how research by linguists and anthropologists had changed the historian's perspective on oral evidence:

> Up to the present in taking evidence of past social conditions we have naturally paid most attention to the content of what our informants told us – chiefly the social conditions they had experienced and their reaction to them. Although, for my part, I was also interested in the actual speech . . . it was chiefly in the words themselves and not particularly in the shape of the language . . . *what* an informant said took precedence over *how* he said it. But in the light of this new [work] increasing value will be placed by

linguists and by anthropologists or students of folk-life on the *form* of a man's [sic] testimony. They will do this if only to test the hypothesis that the unconscious element in a man's speech will, to a certain extent at least, mirror the actual assumptions of the culture in which he lives. (p. 174)

8 Joanna Bornat's article (1989) offers a useful overview of these debates, as do others in the same issue of the *Oral History Journal.*

9 The issue of revealing or concealing matters to do with your political, sexual or moral preferences in teaching is an old one. Because of the construction of 'adult illiterates' as vulnerable people, by implication with no coherent personal or world view of their own, adult literacy work has from time to time been subject to criticism for being dangerously 'political'. One example of this was the case of the worksheets at Brighton Friends Centre in 1977, resulting in newspaper headlines such as 'Left wing bias attack on school for semi-literates' (Mace (1979), p. 25).

10 Ballard and Clanchy (1988) p.11.

11 Yet it is odd how the one demand made of students that we as teachers could, without risk, meet ourselves, is so rarely applied: and that is precisely this demand to *date* and *name* our writing. Countless communication skills workshops and literacy classrooms across the country contain boxes and files of anonymous and timeless worksheets. Rarely do the authors give their name, or even their initials, at the bottom of the sheet: even more rarely do they think to log the moment at which they wrote it.

To any professional historian, a source without a name or date is frustrating and almost useless. If we are to be credible teachers of such a process, and be historians of our own work and our learning, then it follows that names and dates are essential to every piece of paper we ever write for teaching purposes. Then we can see them as the temporal and authored documents they are: just working papers, truths that we have come up with, for now: not absolutes, for all time.

12 Kress (1982).

13 Archer and Costello (1990), p. 167.

14 Freire (1985), p. 2.

15 Hampshire (1991), p. 51.

16 Lawrence and Mace (1987).

17 Britton, J., 'Writing to learn and learning to write' in Pradl (1982), see especially p. 101.

18 Lawrence and Mace, op. cit., p. 22. The description and transcript extract is from a discussion of the Lee Centre's Caribbean History Group, October 1984.

19 Mace (1979), p. 116.

20 Cutts and Maher (1984).

21 Moss (1987b), p. 2.

22 Darville (1989), Lickiss (1988).

23 Neville (1990).

24 Kress, op. cit. p. 98.

25 Smith (1982), p. 10.
26 Fussell (1975), p. 181.
27 Smith, op. cit., p. 23.
28 ALBSU Newsletter no. 40, winter 1991.
29 Thompson (1991), p. 18.
30 I discussed some of the problems in an article called 'Snatch and grab it – community education's cautious promises', Mace (1988b).
31 Walkerdine (1985), p. 2.

CHAPTER 3

1 See for example the accounts of women's non-formal education reported in an international conference in which the forces against such education include the burden of debt and war: World University Service (1991).
2 Wilkinson (1975), pp. 10–12.
3 Loving and Mace (1987).
4 Foster (1980).
5 Armstrong (1982), p. 25, 32.
6 Seebohm Report, *Local authority and allied personal services*, HMSO, 1968.
7 Barton and Padmore (1991), pp. 70, 71.
8 Advisory Council for Adult and Continuing Education (1979), pp. 12–16. Nell Keddie, writing a year later, saw this report as 'the most extreme example we have seen so far of the way that a concept of individual need and student-centredness is used to legitimize an ideological commitment by adult education to the status quo' (Keddie 1980: 62.
9 Hamilton (1987), p. 8.
10 An excellent challenge to this convention is to be found in Ann Oakley's account of her research on the transition to motherhood. She carried out 178 interviews over a period of 12 months. In her analysis of the tape-recordings, she listed no less than 878 questions which interviewees asked her at some point during the interviewing process (three quarters of which were requests for information). She comments: 'It would be the understatement of all time to say that I found it very difficult to avoid answering these questions as honestly and fully as I could' (Oakley, 1980: 50). She also reported that a majority of the women she interviewed had said that they had found the process of being interviewed a positive one, and a means of reflecting on their experience.
11 Bonnerjea (1987), p. 9.
12 Michael Cunningham, in 'Groundwork and ground rules' (Mace and Yarnit 1987: 152–8), argues forcefully for the importance of trade union participation in all workplace training courses. He summarises it bluntly:

All the goody management people in the world – and even all the goody trade union people – will not make much of an impact if we haven't carefully prepared the ground. I am talking here of *outreach work*, to be done by local union activists and adult educationists *working in concert*. (p. 154)

13 From a piece written by a group of former students on Sheffield Council's 'Take Ten' courses, published in Mace and Yarnit (1987), p. 108.
14 Cambridge Training and Development (1988), pp. 16, 48.

CHAPTER 4

1 Holland (1991), pp. 13, 14.
2 For a useful source on the work of these courses see: *TSD Preparatory courses in the 80s* (conference report), London: National Association of Teachers in Further and Higher Education/Assocation for Adult and Continuing Education, 1981.
3 Dallimore (1980).
4 Roz Ivanič's work,

certainly started and ended with practical concerns. It began with a simple practical question to do with punctuation: why do people put full stops where they do? This led her through the research literature on written and spoken language, and on to an investigation of the reasons learners give for their placement of full stops, particulary the 'incorrect' ones. The results of this small study tell us something about the structure of written language; they also have practical implications for how teachers explain punctuation.

(Hamilton and Barton 1985: 52)

5 ILEA Afro-Caribbean Language and Literacy Project in Further Education (1990).
6 Charnley and Jones (1979), p. 2.
7 R.J. Kedney wrote, at the peak of the publicity for the 'adult literacy campaign':

As it has come to be realised that the broadcast material will not of itself teach adults to read or tutors to teach, there has developed an almost frenetic search for new and acceptable guidelines. But in this as in other aspects of this new field of work, definitive answers cannot yet be expected . . . Unless self-questioning of a systematic kind . . . is regularly undertaken there are various obvious dangers. First, that hasty and emotional responses will be made to needs that seem so clearly evident and clamant. Secondly, that once a stance has been taken on any item of policy it may prove very difficult to alter without apparent loss of face. And thirdly, that promises may seem to be held out that are incapable of fulfilment.

(Kedney 1976)

8 I owe this definition to the late Mandy McMahon. I first enjoyed her offering it at the conference on research and practice in adult literacy reported in Hamilton and Barton (1985).

9 Shrapnel Gardener (1984), Introduction, p. 5.
10 See, for instance, Kress (1982) and Docherty (1984).
11 McLaughlin (1985), pp. 8, 10.
12 There are a number of lovely ideas for collecting lists and getting writing started in an anthology of teaching experience by creative writing tutors, Sellers (1991).
13 This course was reported in Ruth Lesirge and Jane Mace, 'Writing and empowerment: women in residence' in *About a week in Nottingham* (1986) International League for Social Commitment in Adult Education (ILSCAE), under the auspices of the National Institute of Adult and Continuing Education, (NIACE).
14 Hamilton and Barton (1985), p. 69.

CHAPTER 5

1 See Ivanic and Moss (1991) for a useful distinction between 'imposed' and 'generated' literacy.
2 See Rainer (1980) for the creative privacy of diary writing.
3 Two other examples of group poems can be found in Mace and Yarnit (1987) pp. 35–6 and Mace (1988b).
4 Richmond (n.d.) p. 7.
5 Nell Keddie has challenged adult education's claims to 'distinctiveness' from the school curriculum by pointing out 'the notion of student-centredness which primary and adult education hold in common' and suggests that if, as the evidence suggests, infant schooling 'tends to produce uniformity rather than diversity', the possibility that this also happens in the curricula of adult education at least bears examining (see Keddie 1980: 53–4).
6 Shrapnel Gardener (1984).
7 Richmond, op. cit., p. 9.
8 I was interested to read a criticism of one use of the widely used 'language experience' in primary school classrooms: Myra Barrs (1987) wrote that the School Council's 'Breakthrough to literacy' scheme was 'notorious for the "I like my" pattern that it frequently generates'. (She went on to suggest that language experience approaches in general 'placed children firmly in the dependent position as writers' – a view which would probably find an equal number of supporters and opponents in adult literacy circles.)
9 See Shrapnel Gardner (1984), Fitzpatrick (1988) for close analysis of peer editorial work.
10 Natalie Goldberg (1986) and Dorothea Brande (1934, repr. 1982) both speak of separating the creative from the critical moments. They are writing, in general, to the individual writer. I think their point applies well to groups, too.
11 Reporting on activities in this country for International Literacy Year, the Adult Literacy and Basic Skills Unit reported that 'perhaps the most important of all writing during the year was student writing, which has been many and varied, and has taken different forms throughout the

153

country', and that, among other student writing activities, 'pen-pal schemes, often with an international dimension, featured strongly' (ALBSU 1990: 24–5).

12 Ruth Lesirge, the colleague in question, has been the author of a number of publications about literacy teaching, particularly teaching methods using visual information: Lesirge and Rothenberg (1984) remains, in my opinion, the most original contribution to a liberatory approach to language and experience for use in English for Speakers of Other Languages (ESOL) and literacy work.

13 These workshops were part of the research for Lawrence and Mace (1991).

CHAPTER 6

1 Molteno (1987), pp. 102, 129.
2 This section is partly based on Mace (1991).
3 Meller (1989).
4 Helen is quoted in Clary (1990).
5 See Bibliography, note on archive sources.
6 *Father's Cap* (1975), published by Cambridge House Literacy Scheme, London, now out of print.
7 FWWCP contact address is: FWWCP, c/o Queenspark Books, 68 Grand Parade, Brighton, BN2 2JY.
8 *Every birth it comes different*, Centerprise, 1980.
9 Mace (1983).
10 The publication (but not the event) is referred to in ALBSU (1990), p. 21.
11 Maureen Cooper, in her study (Cooper 1984) of the power balances of tutor:student and female:male in the editorial meetings of *Write First Time*, found that, while the proportion of female to male members in these meetings was always a majority of female to male, the proportion of tutors to students remained a majority of the first to the second. In short, there were always more women there; and a majority of those women, even after an increase in student participation, were tutors.

In a research study by adult literacy students themselves, planned jointly by tutors and students (reported in Mace and Moss 1988) a total of twenty-six people are listed as participating. The gender composition by student:tutor worked like this:

	student	tutor
male	12	1
female	6	7

The student, who carried out interviews between two project weekends, completed these with a total of 109 people: of whom 63 per cent were men and 37 per cent women.

12 McCaffery (1990).
13 The list was compiled by Sue Shrapnel Gardener, when she was Writing

Development Worker for the Write First Time Organisation (see Bibliography note on archive sources). At the time of writing, Rebecca O'Rourke is working with me on a one-year research project funded by the Leverhulme Trust on student publishing in adult literacy. We intend, in the course of this, to produce a successor to the 1982 list.

14 See, for instance, Charnley and Withnall (1989).

15 See National Federation of Voluntary Education Schemes (1991), Introduction.

16 Buckley, *et al.* (1989), p. 36.

17 Brenda McPherson, *et al.* (eds) (1985) *Education, course, learning, study, teaching. . . TRANSFORMED: collection of writings from the Linked Learning Course*, Hillcroft College (out of print). I am grateful to Ruth Lesirge for raising this point about listening. It was with Ruth that I co-taught the course referred to here, from which this publication emerged.

18 Bown (1990).

19 Clanchy (1979), p. 219.

20 Jane Lawrence and I found work by Jane Root (Root 1986) particularly interesting on this subject in our work on uses of literacy and television (Lawrence and Mace 1991).

21 Tristine Rainer, in a chapter on 'Overcoming writing blocks', distinguishes between the 'Internal Censor', who she sees like 'the judgemental "Parent" in Transactional Analysis who says "You're not OK"', and the 'Internal Critic', who 'constantly judges your writing style'. She says that the way to get round the first is 'remember not to make judgements on yourself while writing'. The Critic has a place, but needs to be kept well away from a first draft. See Rainer (1980), p. 217.

22 Lesirge and Mace (1991) was one effort in this direction.

23 Fitzpatrick (1988), p. 33.

24 John Glynn's comment is extracted from an interview with Sue Shrapnel Gardener in her 'Writing for other people' in Shrapnel Gardener (1984), A12, p. 3.

25 Fitzpatrick, op. cit., p. 28.

26 Duffin (1990), p. 18.

CHAPTER 7

1 See Barton and Ivanič (1991) for examples of different literacy communities.

2 The White Paper, Education and training for the twenty-first century (June 1991) specifically excluded 'adults' leisure interests' from the brief of the single funding council proposed for adult and further education (vol. 1, para. 9.11). The response from the National Institute for Adult and Continuing Education (July 1991) opposed what it called the 'new and equally artificial distinction' between vocational and non-vocational education.

3 NUPE Basic Skills Project, founded in 1978, renamed 'Workbase', had by 1987 worked with 15 different employers in over 30 workplaces,

developing more than 80 workplace-related basic education courses with more than 1,000 employees (Bonnerjea 1987). Their purpose is explicitly to do with identifying 'needs'. These are examples of the two opposing views of employers in relation to the 'need' they perceived for workplace basic education: 'Why are we paying for these people to read and write when they don't need to?'; and, 'We wouldn't hesitate to take operators away from the shopfloor and teach them to operate new machines. What we are doing now has no quantifiable benefit, but we believe that confidence in communication skills is what we have to be about' (Taw 1990).

4 Reported in Mace (1985a).

5 These were derived from a list of categories suggested in a publication I still find useful for ideas about language and literacy in context, Doughty, Pearce and Thornton (1971), p. 55.

6 Ronald Stanford (Stanford, 1981: 170) tells us that a UNESCO committee proposed the definition for census purposes. Their wording was: 'A person is literate who can, with understanding, both read and write a short simple statement on his everyday life.' His comment, in my view, oversimplifies this apparently so simple task; he asserts that the definition 'sets the standard of literacy at the very lowest acceptable level: *it does not require the person concerned to be able to read or write anything beyond a short and simple statement on the most familiar of topics*' [my italics].

7 The conference, 'Towards 1992 . . . education of adults in the new Europe', was organised by the Standing Conference on University Teaching and Research in the Education of Adults (SCUTREA) and held at Sheffield University in July 1990.

8 Levine (1986), p. 162.

9 For the discussion of literacy events, see Street (1984) and Barton and Ivanic (1991).

10 For letter-writing situations, see for example Moss (1986), Turner (1985).

11 Moss (1987a), p. 40 quotes an interesting example described to her by a former 'fresh start' student of the value attributed to such 'role play' work:

> I just don't let things go past now that I would have a few years ago . . . At work my boss is a real 'man' . . . The coffee would come in and if we didn't jump up and get him his coffee he'd say, 'I haven't any coffee – is nobody going to get me some?' And the young ones would jump up and give it to him. Well, we'd practised that situation in one of the classes. . . as a role play, so next time, I said to one of the girls, 'I'm damned if I'm going to get up and give him coffee, let him get his own.' And she agreed . . . Before I would have just jumped up and got it for him.

12 Frank Smith suggests that a fluent speaker of English is likely to speak an average of 200–300 words a minute; and that a fluent writer, in neat handwriting, is unlikely to produce more than 25 words a minute (Smith 1982: 22). New technology and keyboard skills may achieve a

narrowing of this differential. For most of us, selection, scribble and shorthand are still the only solutions.

13 Mace (1981), p. 10.
14 Ken gave me an interview as part of the research I was doing to learn about the perception literacy students had of their experience, published in Mace (1979b).
15 Levine (1986), p. 2.
16 The interview with Daisy was part of the research I did about women and paid educational leave; she is quoted further in Mace and Yarnit (1987), pp. 23–8.

BIBLIOGRAPHY

All publishing locations are London, UK, unless otherwise stated.

Adult Literacy and Basic Skills Unit (1991) *International Literacy Year 1990*, ALBSU.

Advisory Council for Adult and Continuing Education (1979) *A Strategy for the Basic Education of Adults*, Leicester: ACACE.

Ahmad (1990), 'Across the seven seas: Asians in the North East', in *Adults Learning*, vol. 2, no. 1, pp. 22–4.

Archer, D. and Costello, P. (1990) *Literacy and power: the Latin American battleground*, Earthscan.

Armstrong, P. (1982) 'The myth of meeting needs in adult education and community development', in *Critical Social Policy*, vol. 2, no. 2, pp. 24–39.

Ballard, B. and Clanchy, J. (1988) 'Literacy in the University: an "Anthropological" Approach', in Taylor, G. *et al.* (eds) *Literacy by Degrees*, Society for Research in Higher Education/Open University Press, pp. 7–24.

Barrs, M. (1987) 'Learning to write', in *Language Matters*, Centre for Language in Primary Education, pp. 1–2.

Barton, D. and Ivanic, R. (1991) *Writing in the Community*, Sage.

Barton, D. and Padmore, S. (1991) 'Roles, networks and values in everyday writing', in D. Barton and R. Ivanic (eds) *Writing in the Community*, Sage, pp. 58–78.

Baynham, M. and Mace, J. (1986) *Doing Research: Interviews, Tapes and Transcriptions, and Observations*, Lee Centre/Goldsmiths' College.*

Bornat, J. (1989) 'Oral history as a social movement: reminiscence and older people', in *Oral History Journal*, vol. 17, no. 2, pp. 16–26.

Bown, L. (1990) 'Literacy and the liberation of women', in J. Freeland (ed.) *Literacy and liberation: WUS annual conference 1990*, World University Service.

Bonnerjea, L. (1987) *Workbase Trades Union Education and Skills Project: a Research Report*, ALBSU.

Brande, D. (1934, UK repr. 1983) *Becoming a Writer*, Papermac.

British Association of Settlements (1974) *A Right to Read: Action for a Literate Britain*, British Association of Settlements.

Britton, J. (1970) *Language and literacy*, Pelican.

Bryan, B., Dadzie, S. and Scafe, S. (1985) *The Heart of the Race: Black Women's Lives in Britain*, Virago.

Buckley, A., *et al.* (eds) (1989) *Given the chance we can do it*, Dublin: National Literacy Agency.

Cambridge Training and Development Ltd (1988) *Working on Writing*, ALBSU/COIC.

Charnley, A.H. and Jones, H.A. (1979) *The Concept of Success in Adult Literacy*, ALBSU.

Charnley, A.A. and Withnall, A. (1989) *Developments in Adult Basic Education: Special Development Projects 1978–85*, ALBSU.

Clanchy, M. (1979), *From Memory to Written Record: 1066–1307*, Edward Arnold.

Clarke, J. (1989) *'This is a lifetime thing': Outcomes for Adult Basic Education students from Hackney Adult Education Institute and the Hackney Reading Centre*, ALFA, North and East London Open College Network. Clary, H. (1990) 'Reading aloud – or not?', in *ALBSU Newsletter*, no. 39, p. 7.

Cooper, M. (1984) 'Managing the collective Write First Time collectively: an examination of the necessary conditions "every meeting an educational process"', unpublished diploma thesis, *Write First Time* archive.*

Cutts, M. and Maher, C. (1984) *Gobbledygook*, Allen & Unwin.

Dallimore, P. (1978) 'When I leave school', in *Shush – mum's writing*, Bristol: Bristol Broadsides.

Darville, R. (1989) 'The language of experience and the literacy of power', in M. Taylor and J. Draper (eds) *Adult Literacy Perspectives*, Toronto: Culture Concepts Inc.

Department of Education and Science (1991) *Education and Training for the Twenty-first Century*, HMSO, Cm 1356.

Docherty, M. (1984) 'That's not right. Look! There's no Daddy in this book', in J. Miller (ed.) *Eccentric propositions: Essays on Literature and the Curriculum*, Routledge & Kegan Paul.

Doughty, P., Pearce, J., and Thornton, G. (1971) *Language in Use* (Schools Council Project in Linguistics and English Teaching), Arnold.

Duffin, P. (1990) 'A place for personal history in', *Adults Learning*, vol. 2, no. 1, pp. 17–19.

Evans, N. (1984) *Exploiting Experience*, Further Education Unit/PICKUP.

Ewart Evans, G. (1977) *Where Beards Wag All: the Relevance of the Oral Tradition*, Faber & Faber.

Fitzpatrick, S. (1988) *Working around words: an account of editorial work for two Gatehouse books*, Manchester: Gatehouse.

Foster, P. (1980) 'A quiet rush in the Scottish Highlands', in *Basic Education*, no. 3, Cambridge: National Extension College.

Francis, H. (1991) 'Literacy standards and teaching methods' in *Viewpoints 11: The Teaching of Reading*, ALBSU, pp. 2–18.

Freire, P. (1985) *The Politics of Education: Culture, Power and Liberation* Massachusetts: Bergin & Harvey.

Freire, P. and Shor, I. (1987) *A Pedagogy for Liberation: Dialogues on Transforming Education*, Macmillan.

Fussell, P. (1975) *The Great War and Modern Memory*, Oxford: OUP.

Gerry (1983) 'I felt I was the only person in this whole great metropolis who ever had this problem', in *Where do we go from here? Adult lives without literacy*, Manchester: Gatehouse, pp. 21–7.

Goldberg, N. (1986), *Writing down the bones: freeing the writer within*, Boston and London: Shambala.

Graff, H. (1979) *The Literacy Myth: Literacy and Social Structure in the 19th century city*, New York: Academic Press.

Gregory, G. (1984) 'Using community published writing in the classroom', in J. Miller, (ed.) *Eccentric propositions: essays on literature and the curriculum*, Routledge & Kegan Paul.

Gregory, G. (1991) 'Community publishing as self education', in D. Barton and R. Ivanic (eds) *Writing in the Community*, Sage, pp. 109–42.

Hamadache, A., and Martin, D. (1986) *Theory and Practice of Literacy Work: Policies, Strategies and Examples*, Paris: UNESCO/CODE.

Hamilton, M. (1987) *Literacy, Numeracy and Adults: Evidence from the National Child Development Study*, ALBSU.

Hamilton, M. and Barton, D. (1985) *Research and Practice in Adult Literacy* (papers of the Association of Recurrent Education), Nottingham: ARE, University of Nottingham.

Hampshire, S. (1991) *Every Letter Counts: Winning in Life Despite Dyslexia*, Corgi.

Hautecoeur, J.-P. (1990) 'Generous supply, flagging demand: the current paradox of literacy', in J.-P. Hautecoeur (ed.) *Alpha 90: Current Research in Literacy*, Paris: UNESCO, pp. 113–33.

Holland, D. (1989) *The Progress Profile: Assessment of Student Progress in Adult Literacy*, Nottingham: University of Nottingham.

ILEA Afro-Caribbean Language and Literacy Project in Further and Adult Education (1990) *Language and Power*, Harcourt Brace Jovanovich.

Ivanič, R. and Moss, W. (1991), 'Bringing community writing practices into education', in D. Barton and R. Ivanic, *Writing in the community*, Sage, pp. 193–224.

Keddie, N. (1980) 'Adult education: an ideology of individualism', in J. Thompson (ed.) *Adult Education for a Change*, Hutchinson, pp. 45–65.

Kedney, R. (1976) 'Educational objectives in adult literacy provision' in *Studies in Adult Education*, vol. 8, no. 1, pp. 1–14.

Kress, G. (1982), *Learning to Write*, Routledge & Kegan Paul.

Lawrence, J. and Mace, J. (1986) *Remembering in Groups: Ideas from Literacy and Reminiscence Work*, Oral History Society.

—— (1991) *Television, Talk and Writing: Issues for Discussion with Adult Students* Cambridge: National Extension College.

Lesirge, R. and Mace, J. (1987) 'Women, part-time study and release', in *Newsletter of the European Bureau of Adult Education*, summer issue.

—— (1989) *Pass us the Map: a Study of Women's Education in New Zealand*, ILEA Camden Institute.

—— (1991) 'Read this and pass this on: writing, academics and managers', in *Adults Learning*, April issue, pp. 236–8.

Lesirge, R. and Rothenburg, S. (1983) *Images and Understanding*, Cambridge: National Extension College.

Levine, K. (1986) *The Social Context of Literacy*, Routledge & Kegan Paul.

Lickiss, R. (1988) *Providing Information about Public Services: Studies of the Effectiveness of Written and Spoken Information*, Brighton:Lewis Cohen Urban Studies Centre, Brighton Polytechnic.

Loewenstein, A. (1983) 'Teaching writing in prison', in C. Bunch and S. Pollack, (eds) *Learning our way: Essays in Feminist Education*, New York: Crossing Press, pp. 34–48.

Loving, S. and Mace, J. (1987) 'Literacy: how can we talk about it? a report on a workshop for local advice and community workers', in *ALBSU Newsletter*, no. 26, pp. 6–7.

McCaffery, J. (1990) 'Ideology and curriculum', in B. Street (ed.) *Literacy in Development: People, Language and Power* (report of seminar organised by Education for Development, Commonwealth Institute and British Association for Literacy in Development (BALID)), BALID, pp. 54–9.

McCaffery, J., and Street, B. (1988) *Literacy Research in the UK: Adult and School Perspectives*, Lancaster: RaPAL.

Mace, J. (1975) 'Blaming the victim', in *Times Educational Supplement*, 30 May 1975, pp. 18–19.

—— (1979a) 'Sensationalism or sound sense? – adult literacy in context', *Assistant Librarian*, May issue.

—— (1979b) *Working with Words: Literacy Beyond School*, Writers & Readers.

—— (1979c) 'Rewriting literature: publishing out of adult literacy', *Oral History Journal*, autumn issue, pp. 63–7.

—— (1980) *Learning from Experience: Discussion and Materials for Adult Groups Studying the Uses of Language, Literacy and Communication*, Adult Literacy Support Services Fund; now Broadcasting Support Services.

—— (1981) 'Watch your language: the politics of literacy now' *Red Letters*, December issue, pp. 2–13.

—— (1983) 'Women talking: Feminism and Adult Literacy Work', *Frontiers: Journal of Women's Studies*, vol. 7, no. 1, pp. 38–43.

—— (1985a) *A Time and a Place: a Study of Education and Manual Work*, Lee Centre/Goldsmiths' College.

—— (1985b) 'Students in control: objects and subjects', in D. Barton and M. Hamilton (eds) *Research and Practice in Adult Literacy*, Nottingham: Association for Recurrent Education, pp. 60–8.

—— (1986) 'Time for recognition: adults studying literacy', *Teaching London Kids*, no. 24, pp. 20–1.

——(1988a) 'Privacies made public' *Booknews*, no. 2, April issue, pp. 2–4.

——(1988b) 'Snatch and grab it: community education's cautious promises', *Journal of Community Education*, vol. 7, no. 1, pp. 26–8.

——(1991) '"Trust grew, and so did we": reflections from the UK', in L. Limage (ed.) *Literacy and the Role of the University*, Paris: UNESCO, pp. 62–9.

Mace, J. and Moss, W. (1988) *How do People Decide to Join a Literacy Class? the Report of a Research Study by Literacy Students*, Lee Centre/

Goldsmiths' College in association with the National Federation of Voluntary Education Schemes.

Mace, J. and Wolfe, M. (1988) 'Women, work and release' *Adult Education* vol. 61, no. 1, pp. 49–54.

—— (1990) 'Identity, authorship and status: some issues for the UK from International Literacy Year', *Adults Learning*, June issue, pp. 264–6.

Mace, J. and Yarnit, M. (1987) *Time off to Learn: Paid Educational Leave and Low Paid Workers*, Methuen.

McLaughlin, J. (1985) 'Creative writing in second language work', in *Viewpoints: Literacy and Second Language Speakers of English*, ALBSU.

Meller, D. (1989) 'Where do we go from here', in I. Bild (ed.) *Once I Was a Washing Machine*, Federation of Worker Writers and Community Publishers, pp. 88–96.

Molteno, M. (1987) *A Language in Common*, The Women's Press.

Moss, W. (1984) 'Why are meetings hard?', in *Putting you in the Picture: Lee Centre Report 1984*, Lee Centre/Goldsmiths' College.

—— (1986) *Writing Letters*, Cambridge: National Extension College.

—— (1987a) *Breaking the Barriers: Eight Case Studies of Women Returning to Learning in North London*, ALFA/Polytechnic of North London.

—— (1987b) 'The Plain English Campaign: an overview', *RaPAL Bulletin*, no. 4, pp. 1–6.

Naughton, B. (1961, repr. 1974) 'Maggie's first reader', in *The Goalkeeper's Revenge*, Puffin, pp. 112–19.

National Federation of Voluntary Education Schemes (1991) *'If it Wasn't for the Second Chance'*, NFVES.

Oakley, A. (1981) 'Interviewing women: a contradiction in terms', in H. Roberts (ed.) *Doing Feminist Research*, Routledge & Kegan Paul, pp. 30–61.

Pradl, G. M. (ed.) (1982) *Prospect and Retrospect: Selected Essays of James Britton*, Montclair, NJ: Boynton/Cook.

Rainer, T. (1980) *The New Diary*, Australia: Angus & Robertson.

Richmond, J. (1991), 'A policy for writing', in J. Richmond, *et al.* (eds), *The English Curriculum: Writing – Material for Discussion*, English Centre.

Root, J. (1986) *Open the Box*, Comedia.

Sellers, S. (ed.) (1991) *Taking Reality by Surprise: Writing for Pleasure and Publication* Women's Press.

Shrapnel Gardener, S. (1979) 'Thoughts on paper: publications from adult literacy centres, 1974–78' *Adult Education Journal*, July issue.

—— (1985) *Conversations with Strangers*, ALBSU/Write First Time.

Smith, F. (1982) *Writing and the writer*, Heinemann.

Stanford, R. (1981) 'Language and adult education, with special emphasis on adult literacy' in L. Bown, and J.T. Okedara (eds) *An Introduction to the Study of Adult Education*, Ibadan: Ibadan University Press, pp. 168–85.

Street, B. (1984) *Literacy in Theory and Practice*, Cambridge: Cambridge University Press.

—— (1991) 'Putting literacies on the political agenda' *Open Letter: Australian Journal for Adult Literacy Research and Practice* vol. 1, no. 1, pp. 5–16.

Taw, R. (1990) 'Basic skills in the workplace' *ALBSU Newsletter no. 38* (insert).

Turner, M. (1985) *Literacy Work with Bilingual Students*, ILEA/ALBSU.

UNESCO (1990) *ILY: Year of Opportunity*, Paris: ILY Secretariat of UNESCO.

Walkerdine, V. (1985) 'On the regulation of speaking and silence: subjectivity, class and gender in contemporary schooling', in C. Steedman, C. Urwin and V. Walkerdine, *Language, Gender and Childhood*, Routledge & Kegan Paul.

Waring, M. (1988) *Counting for Nothing: What Men Value and What Women are Worth*, Wellington NZ: Allen & Unwin.

Wickert, R. (1989) *No Single Measure: A Survey of Autralian Adult Literacy*, Sydney: Sydney College of Advanced Education.

Wilkins, M. (1990) 'Moving away from "Needs",' *Language Issues*, vol. 4, no. 1.

Wilkinson, K. (1975) 'Short story of my life', *Write First Time*, vol. 4, no. 4, p. 4. *

World University Service (WUS) (1991) *Aid and Women's Non-formal Education*, World University Service.

* *Note on Archive sources*. Papers published by the 'Write First Time' between 1975–85 and publications by the Lee Community Education Centre (abbreviated to Lee Centre) between 1980–91, are no longer in print. Both organisations have lodged comprehensive archives of their work, which are available for consultation: Write First Time at the library of Ruskin College, Oxford; and the Lee Community Education Centre at the library of Goldsmiths' College, University of London. In both cases, researchers are requested to contact the librarian to make an appointment to view the material.

INDEX

164